Jes
God loves u
walk in holy
boldness and
fearless faith.

♡ Yvette
10/2017

*Being Ruth: Pressing Through Life's Struggles with Fearless Faith*
©2017 by Yvette R. Blair-Lavallais. All rights reserved.

Published by Her Sisters Situation Ministries

ISBN 13: 978-0-9990216-0-6
ISBN 10: 0-9990216-0-5

Cover Design: Christoper Thomas of Chris Thomas Graphics
Interior Design: Brandi K. Etheredge
Copy Editor: Yvette R. Blair-Lavallais

"This beautifully crafted resource has challenged me to the core of my being. Yvette Blair-Lavallais has managed to handle a familiar story, untangle its threads, and weave them into my own story in a profound way. Rarely have I encountered a book that traces the sisterhood of the faith so powerfully, from Naomi and Ruth to Sojourner Truth to my own life. This isn't just a must-read, it's a must re-read."

**Elizabeth Glass Turner,** Associate Director of Community and Creative Development, World Methodist Evangelism

"Yvette's vivid, practical, and contemporary style provides a fresh and encouraging look at the ancient story of Ruth. Readers, especially women, will walk away from this book with hope and encouragement that God will see them through their journey just as He did in this powerful and compelling story of our sister Ruth."

**Rev. Velda M. Turnley,** Chief Encouragement & Empowerment Officer, Kingdom Impact Now Global Solutions, Staff Pastor, St. Luke Community UMC Dallas, TX

*Being Ruth: Pressing Through Life's Struggles with Fearless Faith* is a book that is life changing. You will be moved to a place of applying your faith to the ongoing "midst of life" dynamics and the practice of a relevant faith. The interplay of Yvette's life experiences and the rich content from the story of Ruth, create a reading experience that makes the book of Ruth truly come alive. It is a relevant text and book for those that face the many and varied struggles of everyday life.

**Rev. Rezolia Johnson Roberson**
Senior Pastor, Church of the Covenant
Arlington, TX

In *Being Ruth: Pressing Through Life's Struggles with Fearless Faith*, Yvette Blair-Lavallais takes the relationship between Ruth and Naomi from the pages of the Bible and makes their trials and triumphs applicable to contemporary times. Through the individual and collective stories of these courageous women, Yvette offers how relationship with God, especially during seasons of drought, unlocks the door of encouragement, hope and God's promise in your life. Whatever struggles you're facing, this book will help you to be restored.

**Candance L. Greene**
Founder, Cherishedflight Ministry
Baltimore, MD

# Being Ruth

## Pressing Through Life's Struggles with Fearless Faith

### YVETTE R. BLAIR-LAVALLAIS

# Table of Contents

# *Dedication*

This book is dedicated to my mother, Tonnette Blair, who was my best friend, confidante and nurturing supporter. Long before congestive heart failure claimed her life, causing her to take her very last breath in 2014, she modeled and exemplified for me what it means to have strength, courage, and unwavering faith no matter whatever season you are in. The Book of Ruth was one of her favorite books in the Bible and we spent a lot of time studying it and looking at ways in which God was speaking to us through such a beautiful and illustrative story. I am glad that she had an opportunity to see the blueprint for this book when I first began writing it in 2013. As a candidate for ordained ministry in The United Methodist Church, I was required to develop and write a Bible study and present it to the Board of Ordained Ministry before being commissioned as a provisional elder.

# Acknowledgments

To my sisters, Yolonda and Harriett, and my big brother, Clifford, we have pressed our way through many struggles, not the least of which was losing our mother and our brother, Barriett, in the same year. To my niece, Nariana, a brilliant engineer and word-bearer of the Gospel, never underestimate the plans that God has for your life. Watch with expectancy of how your gifts will intersect for God's glory as you bless so many people.

To my amazing husband, teaching and preaching pastor, Carl, thank you for your encouragement, love and support. Most of all, thank you for the sacrifices that you have made so that we can both proclaim God's word in sacred spaces, whether it is in the pulpit or in publications.

To the faith community at Bethel AME Church in Dallas where I spent my pre-school years in the days before every learning tool and toy had an ISB port, a battery or an online application associated with it, thank you for helping to raise me to be a girl of faith who grew into a woman of faith. To the faith community at Lee Chapel AME Church in Dallas where I sat as a little girl with my family and Godmother, Geraldine Henry, and heard the voice of God calling me to something greater than myself. It was there that my calling into ministry was surely being formed. You will always be my "home church" because this is where church became home for me.

To the faith community at The Antioch Church in Dallas, First Christian Methodist Evangelistic Church in Dallas, The Woods United Methodist Church in Grand Prairie, The St. Luke

"Community" United Methodist Church in Dallas, and Grace UMC in Arlington, thank you for your support, prayers and enthusiasm for the ministry that we shared together through bible studies, Sunday messages, women's events and fellowship-ping. You have helped to shape my ministry in amazing and meaningful ways.

To my After The Music Stops family - Rev. Russell St. Bernard, Brandi Etheredge and Chris Thomas, we have worked on many projects together over the years. Thank you for your creative gift-edness in helping me to produce this work. May God bless you beyond measure and continue to enrich your gifts for ministry.

To my besties: Candance L, Rezolia L, and Jill M, thank you for your unwavering friendship. And to all my aunts and my cousins, our family roots run deep in grit, determination and fearless faith!

# Introduction

Have you ever beamed with excitement about an opportunity to do something new? Something like relocating to a different city for a better job, launching a personal campaign to get more involved in community engagement, going back to school for a certification, license or degree, and then after some time had passed, you found yourself second-guessing the opportunity because your situation changed and things were no longer exciting and fulfilling? There was a defining moment in your life that caused everything to change. You went from feeling the anticipation of what was ahead to the anxiety of what was before you. Life presented a situation where everything seemed to have slowly edged toward frustration, disappointment and a real sense of unsettledness. And your faith was damaged in the process. You went from being full of hope and faith to an all-time low of hoped-out and a level of faith that could best be described as "barely hanging on." Trying to press your way through it proved to be the biggest battle of your life. The truth is, you might still be in it right now. You have found yourself stuck between a rock and a hard place, and the more you try to make sense of things, the harder it seems to emerge from that place. And just when it feels like the weight of the situation is stronger than your spiritual life, more formidable than your faith, you make a decision that will either move you forward or send you on a snap-back spiral to more of the same disappointment, spiritual fatigue and unrest. *That's your defining moment.*

Rest assured that you are in good company because the same was true for Naomi. She had a defining moment in her faith journey that knocked her off her feet and caused her to cry aloud in anguish to God. Ruth had a defining moment, too. She was a young woman who didn't have any experience with God until she saw what happened to her mother-in-law, Naomi. She knew that she had two choices before her: fall back to her old faithless lifestyle or press through one of the toughest seasons of her life, choosing to trust in God with an attitude of fearless faith. Ruth's defining moment forever changed the trajectory of the very foundation of our Christian faith. Had it not been for her fearless faith, she would not have divinely met her husband and given birth to their son, which started the lineage that led to the birth of her great-grand-son King David. She represents today's woman of God, who didn't just know *of* God, or hear *about* God from her mother-in-law, or one of the other elders in the family, but came to "know God for herself."

It is my prayer that this exploration into the story of Ruth will help you to "know God for yourself," and discover that God's love is transformational. It is so easy to get caught up in the situations that cause you to be fearful, but God wants you to be like Ruth and have a fearless faith! This book will help you to rise above your doubts and fears and to walk boldly in your faith in Christ. It will help you to see your situations as stepping stones toward your future instead of casting them as setbacks to your past. It is when your circumstances look like they are at their bleakest, that God is encouraging you to ramp up your dependence on God and to declare that you will move from fearful to fearless.

This book will help you to uncover the "fearless faith" that is inside of you. The kind of faith that will help you to press through the struggles of life and to produce the life that God desires for you. The kind of faith that will minimize your doubts about your situation and instead increase your dependence on the God who is your Savior in every situation. Get ready for *your* defining moment. This is your invitation to be vulnerable and transparent before the Lord with whatever you are dealing with so that you can learn how to press through life's struggles with fearless faith.

# CHAPTER ONE

# Hardships Help You to Hold On

*"In the days when the judges ruled, there was a famine in the land, and a certain man of Bethlehem in Judah went to live in the country of Moab, he and his wife and two sons. The name of the man was Elimelech and the name of his wife, Naomi, and the names of his two sons were Mahlon and Chilion; they were Ephrathites from Bethlehem in Judah. They went into the country of Moab and remained there. But Elimelech, the husband of Naomi, died and she was left with her two sons. These took Moabite wives; the name of the one was Orpah and the name of the other Ruth. When they had lived there about ten years, both Mahlon and Chilion also died, so that the woman was left without her two sons and her husband."*
*— Ruth 1:1-5 —*

When my sister was sixteen, my mother took her to the Department of Motor Vehicles to get her driver's license. This wasn't the usual teenager-issued license where you are required to have an adult over the age of eighteen in the car with you. This was a special license that, in those days, could only be issued at the discretion of a municipal judge. It was called a "hardship" license and was issued only when there was proof of an unusual economic hardship on the family of a minor. There had to be some extenuating circumstances of the parent as a prerequisite for the judge to say yes. Simply put, it had to be a condition that was difficult to endure. My mother had to show proof of her hardship in order for my sister to be allowed to have a driver's license that allowed her to drive without the restrictions of being accompanied by an adult and without the restrictions of driving only between the hours of 8am and 8pm.

My sister was actively involved in sports in high school. She was on the volleyball, basketball, and track team. And she played clarinet in the marching band. And she competed in the academic decathlons. With all the practices and rehearsals in the early mornings and late evenings, there was no way that our mother could drive her to each one. It became increasingly clear that we were faced with a need for my sister to be able to drive herself to school, practice, games, track meets, and band competitions. My mother had two choices: she could either pull my sister from all these extra-curricular activities, or she could make my sister pick one. Rather than deny my sister the opportunity to participate in these events, my mother decided to go before a judge and seek a hardship license for my sister. After all, our situation met the requirements for what the court deemed a hardship. My mother was divorced, and raising me and my siblings alone. The judge commended my mother for working as hard as she did as a single mom, and for supporting my sister's academic interests, and he complimented my sister on her academic and sports achievements.

After recognizing that we had a legitimate dilemma, the judge granted the request and he approved the issuance of a hardship driver's license for my sister. There was one caveat: he needed to know who taught my sister to drive and who would be responsible for her as a driver. Well, my mother had the kind of driver's license, a CDL, that permitted her to drive commercial vehicles, and she had earned the "one million

miles with no accident" driver's award. She accepted responsibility for my sister and understood that this hardship came
with some conditions. My sister was not permitted to have
other teens in the car while she drove and she was not permitted to go "joy riding." It was a condition that my mother was
willing to say yes to so that my sister's school life didn't have
to suffer. Saying yes also meant that my mother didn't have
to adjust her work schedule to be around
to take my sister to all these activities. My
mother was seeking to make things a little
easier for us. And things were going a little
easier until about the fourth month when,
on our way to school one morning, my

*If you change the
way you look at your
circumstances, your
hardships can actually
help you to hold on.*

sister and I were involved in a collision. As we rounded a curve,
a car was stalled in the right-hand lane, and within a matter
of minutes, the car that we were in, severely rear-ended the
other car. My mother's 1977 Cougar XR7 was totaled. And my
sister knew she was toast!

My sister and I were ok. We were more shaken up and
afraid than hurt. Here was my mother, the sole provider of
our family, doing what she could so that we could enjoy a better life. She made this important decision to seek a hardship
driver's license for my sister, and now things had drastically
changed. This move toward a better life was bringing hard
times. My family was temporarily without a car and all of us
were impacted. Not only did my sister not have a way to get
to her extra-curricular activities, but my mother was now impacted in how she would get to work every day.

Talk about extenuating circumstances!

Wouldn't it be something if when life's situations caused
you to experience hardships, you'd be permitted a special license to navigate your way through it? It can easily seem like
hardships can knock the wind out of you and leave you help-
less, but if you change the way you look at your circumstances,
your hardships can actually help you to hold on.

In the opening passage of Ruth, we quickly learn that a hardship has not only hit a "certain" man and his family, but it has hit the very land in which they live. This is hardship multiplied exponentially. It's hardship at a whole "nother" level and the impact is significant. So already we have a crisis. There is a famine in the land and a certain man decides that he and his family will leave Judah and go live in the country of Moab. To say that these were extenuating circumstances is an understatement. Elimelech wasn't relocating his family simply because he was looking for better employment or had landed a new job with great benefits. He moved his family because a famine had hit his hometown. This means that there was no food. The livestock had been depleted. The farmland had dried up. And life went from thriving to barely surviving. Elimelech had to make a life decision. His life and his family's life depended on it.

The text doesn't give us the day-to-day account of Elimelech's life. We don't know the personal struggles that he went through to pack up his belongings, leave his Bethlehem faith community, and move to a new community where God wasn't worshipped as the sovereign Lord. We don't know how this impacted his prayer life, how it grieved him to leave his friends and the people with whom he was accustomed to being in fellowship with and breaking bread. Where did his friends go? Did they try to stick it out a little longer or did they relocate to another town? We have no idea how many nights he stayed up wishing things were better, hoping that the next morning would bring a shift in his circumstances, or how many times he called on the name of God to show up in his situation. We don't know. But we do know that he was in a tough season of life, facing probably one of his greatest struggles as a man, as a provider, as a husband and as a dad.

Before we go any further, place yourself in this situation and imagine what it would mean for you to have to move, unwillingly, because things were so bad in your hometown. Think about the relationships that you would have to leave behind. The places that you frequent. Imagine the restaurants that you love to go to on the weekend. Consider the grocery store that you visit every other week. Life as you know it is changing drastically and as you watch these businesses close because of a sour economic climate, the impact is so devastating that you have to move 40 to 50 miles away just to survive. That was the distance from Bethlehem to Moab. Think about where you live now and identify a town nearly 50 miles away, smaller in population, and lacking amenities and luxuries. Now, consider that the only way to get there is to take a route that doubles or even triples the distance because the terrain that you have to cross is not suitable for walking. You have to navigate your way through grassland, around the Dead Sea, round the wilderness and then get to your destination. That's what it took to get from Bethlehem to Moab.

If you're single, it's hard enough to pick up and start over, especially if you're doing it because *you have to*, rather than want to. You're leaving your support system, perhaps even a person you are dating, and your friends. If you have a family that depends on you, the weight of the decision is magnified because everyone is unhappy and impacted. And the fingers of blame are pointed in your direction. That's heavy.

Now imagine the situation from a faith perspective. You are moving to a community where there is no place to participate in Christian worship. No church building to gather with other Christians and sing God's praises. No faith community where you can leave your burdens at the altar and pray. Instead, you are surrounded by non-believers who practice a lifestyle that is acceptably immoral. *Acceptably immoral*. That's even heavier.

In other words, there are layers to this move that Elimelech had to make. All of this isn't included in the narrative of the story, but it is certainly implied. And that's a lot to contend with – for anybody. In just two verses after we're introduced to

Elimelech, his wife and their two sons, something very tragic happens – Elimelech, this man from Bethlehem, dies. We don't know the cause. We don't know how soon it happened after he arrived in Moab; nor do we know anything about the circumstances surrounding his death. Actually, we don't have to know *what* happened; just knowing that it *did* happen is painful enough. And a flood of emotions begins to rise up in us just knowing this.

We begin to bear witness to the pain that his wife, Naomi, must have been experiencing. She was now a widow. Certainly, she had already gone through the range of emotions from having been a happy and content help mate to her husband and doting mother to their two sons, to being unsettled and frustrated from having to be uprooted so that her family could move to a faithless community called Moab. Can you imagine what that scene must have been like when Elimelech told her that the family had to move? We can only imagine that Naomi's response was punctuated with many, "wait, you said Moab?" exclamations.

Moab is first mentioned in Genesis and carries with it a spiritual stench.

> [30]*Now Lot went up out of Zoar and settled in the hills with his two daughters, for he was afraid to stay in Zoar; so he lived in a cave with his two daughters.* [31]*And the firstborn said to the younger, 'Our father is old, and there is not a man on earth to come in to us after the manner of all the world.* [32]*Come, let us make our father drink wine, and we will lie with him, so that we may preserve offspring through our father.'* [33]*So they made their father drink wine that night; and the firstborn went in, and lay with her father; he did not know when she lay down or when she rose.* [34]*On the next day, the firstborn said to the younger, 'Look, I lay last night with my father; let us make him drink wine tonight also; then you go in and lie with him, so that we may preserve offspring through our father.'* [35]*So they*

*made their father drink wine that night also; and the younger rose, and lay with him; and he did not know when she lay down or when she rose. ³⁶ Thus both the daughters of Lot became pregnant by their father. ³⁷ The firstborn bore a son, and named him Moab; he is the ancestor of the Moabites to this day. ³⁸ The younger also bore a son and named him Ben-ammi; he is the ancestor of the Ammonites to this day.*
— Genesis 19: 30–38. —

Reading this passage gives us some context of what it means for an Israelite living in the land of Bethlehem to leave and live in Moab. It was a bad start to begin with, yet it is also the place where Elimelech relocates his family because it provides what they need immediately: food for survival. It seemed like a place of promise. A place where Elimelech and his family could regroup until things got better in their homeland.

*There are situations in life that will cause you to make some tough decisions.*

For an unpredictable length of time. Elimelech never foresaw what *could* and *would* happen there.

There are situations in life that will cause you to make some tough decisions. Those decisions come with all the "what ifs" that you can imagine. What if you stay where you are? What if things eventually get better? What if things get worse? What if you move and things actually do turn out well? This is where faith in God is so important. You can't predict what tomorrow looks like, but if you are a person of faith, and you act on that faith, then you know without a doubt that God

*When it feels like it's just you against the world, you will discover that God is just a prayer away.*

will be there to meet you in your tomorrow – no matter what it looks like. When you experience a hardship, it can help you to hold on. Yes, you read that right: a hardship can help you to hold on. A hardship can produce a healthy prayer life in you. It is when things go wrong and are at their worst, that you ramp up your prayer life. The longer your season of hardship, the healthier your prayer life becomes. When it feels like it's just you against the world, you will discover that God is just a prayer away. Even if you have never uttered a prayer before, your willingness to recognize that you need to depend on God is all you need to simply say, "Lord help." These two words open the gate for your flood of emotions to flow. These two words uncap the anxiety and the fear that you might be experiencing. These two words can remove the barriers to ramping up your prayer life.

Hardships can also help you to keep your faith tank filled. When you know that the possibility of a long road is ahead of you, having a full tank of faith is essential for the journey. A few years ago, I was driving from Dallas to Lubbock, a town about seven hours away in the western part of Texas, to attend a conference. Part of leaving a metropolis like Dallas where the city is sprawling with activity, excitement and busyness is knowing that I have to shift my thinking, and mentally prepare for the unexpected changes of what it looks like driving through and to small towns. In a big city like Dallas, with a population of more than one million, I am accustomed to seeing high-rise apartments, plush green parks, eclectic shopping areas, restaurants, and heavily-populated neighborhoods. And there is no shortage of gas stations. In fact, at some intersections, there are two or three gas stations, a sign of the convenience of life in a big city.

After about two hours of driving, that reality changed for me. And after about four hours of driving westward, I had to mentally prepare for what was ahead. I saw windmills, cattle, beautiful landscapes, colorful plants and homes peppered along the way. At a certain point of the journey, though, the drive became less and less scenic. I began to wonder if driving to the conference was a mistake. What if I had gotten on the wrong road? What if I couldn't pick up a cell phone signal? A few more miles down the road, I saw a giant billboard that read: "Last gas station for 50 miles." This was a "sign" that I needed to check and make sure that my tank was full. This was a sign informing me that if I didn't stop now to fill up my car, I could easily find myself in a situation where I might run out of gas and be stranded along the road of rolling tumbleweeds. Though my dashboard showed that I had more than a half tank of gas, I knew that the possibility of encountering construction, slow-moving trucks, or even cattle crossing, could impede my journey.

*Sometimes, we approach situations in life with half a tank of faith.*

Sometimes, we approach situations in life with half a tank of faith. We don't replenish our faith tanks daily. Just like a car needs fuel to go, our faith life needs to be refueled. The only way to operate on a full tank of faith is by reading God's word, by meditating on God's promises, by praying, and by spending time in God's presence, simply listening for what God has to say. Daily. If we only do these things on Sunday, we cannot expect that Sunday's time will carry us through the week. It's like eating a great Sunday family meal with baked chicken, fresh spinach, creamy mashed potatoes, buttered rolls, corn on the cob and sweet potato pie, and not eating again for the next six days because this meal is somehow supposed to sustain you until Sunday comes again. Circumstances and situations don't work like that. And neither does faith. Your hardship might not immediately change, but the way you approach it, *through faith*, can change.

Hardships will still cause you to have to make some tough decisions, but if you make the decisions undergirded with faith in God and dependence on God, then you can press through whatever you are going through. Naomi pressed through for more than ten years in a land where she lost her husband, lost her two sons, and to some extent, lost the essence of who she was. That decade of her life was a defining moment. It was a decade of indifference. A decade of distress. A decade of a dark and damming time. A decade of trying to reinvent herself following each tragic loss of her family members. But Naomi pushed her way through it. Even though there was much calamity in Naomi's life – and a whole lot of loss – it is important to note that she didn't bear it alone. For what it's worth, Naomi had two daughters-in-law who were determined to stay with her. These two young women lost a lot, too. They lost their husbands, their societal status and their identification. In biblical times, a woman's identity was tied to either being the daughter of, or the wife of a man. Without that connection, the woman had no social identity. When death hit this family, these three women went from being wives one day to being widows that evening.

Whoa. From wives to widows in one fell swoop.

*You managed to hold on during the worst of your hardships.*

Between these three women, there was a collective grief that took its toll.

For what it's worth, you are not alone. Whatever your setback has been this year, the last few years, or even a decade, it is important to note that someone was there encouraging you – whether you wanted to accept the encouragement or not. Someone was praying for you, whether you ever saw a bowed head and eyes closed – because your own head was bowed so low in despair and grief. Someone was there cheering for you – whether you could hear the hoorah in the distance or the whisper of it up close. More so, God is the "someone" who was there for you and kept the path illumined for you. Even in those darkest moments, God's light still shone through the bouts of weeping, the fits of anger, the pangs of loneliness. You managed to hold on during the worst of your hardships. You made it through a famine – a famine of loss, a famine of few friends, a famine of spiritual unrest, a famine of unemployment, and a famine of faith. Yes, there was a famine in your land. But that teeny, tiny ounce of faith that was hovering deep inside of you – a faith that on some days you weren't even sure was still there – is what kept you holding on during your hardships.

# Be Fearless
## REFLECTION QUESTIONS

**What sign has God been showing you during this season of hardship?**

_____

_____

_____

_____

_____

**Pray and seek God's direction for what action you need to take to press through your hardship. Write down the steps that you will take toward your God-directed action (e.g. spending time in devotion, praying, etc.).**

_____

_____

_____

_____

_____

# CHAPTER TWO

# She Had Grit

*"Go back each of you to your mother's house. May the Lord deal kindly with you, as you have dealt with the dead and with me. The Lord grant that you may find security, each of you in the house of your husband."*
*— Ruth 1:8 —*

For all that Naomi had gone through, she still managed to offer a word of hope and encouragement to her two daughters-in-law. Even though her situation had gotten about as low as low could get, she made the difficult decision to not only return home, but to do so alone. She didn't know what awaited her back in the land of Judah. Other than hearing that the Lord had returned food to the land, Naomi knew that there was no way to know what the outlook was; yet it was an outlook that she was willing to endure, but not one that she wanted Orpah and Ruth to endure.

In the midst of her own pain, uncertainty, and saltiness toward God, Naomi had grit. She made a declaration to these two young women, who still had many years of life ahead of them, to choose the familiar over the unknown – by returning to their mother's house. Naomi knew that she was not in a position to offer any security for her daughters-in-law future. She had a heart-to-heart, woman-to-woman kind of talk with them when she explained that even if she remarried and got pregnant that night, it wouldn't be prudent for them to wait to see if she'd have two more sons whom Orpah and Ruth could marry.

*Life doesn't press a pause button where our hopes catch up with our circumstances.*

That would be ridiculous and unreasonable. Life doesn't press a pause button where our hopes catch up with our circumstances.

Let's be real here – Naomi didn't have anything for herself, yet she cared enough about Orpah and Ruth that she gave them the only thing that she had remaining – encouragement. Sometimes, our circumstances can be so devastating, that we can feel like we don't have anything to offer. But this scene in Naomi's life reminds us that there are times when we have to speak encouragement over our lives. We have to speak encouragement over our situation. We have to be bold enough and fearless enough to press through our situation with a mindset that promotes hope and determination.

It is what happens next that amazes me. Naomi speaks a blessing over Orpah and Ruth. She says, "May the Lord deal kindly with you, as you have dealt with the dead and with me." How you handle your relationships in the midst of your stressful season of life is important because God will honor you for the way you have honored others. If you are unemployed or underemployed because of cutbacks at your job, you still need to honor your relationships with your spouse, children, parents, friends, etc. They did not cause your situation and they should not be mistreated because of your situation. Yes, there will be some dynamics that change within the relationship. You might not be able to spend lavishly on gifts, or provide financial support in areas that you once did, but you can still maintain your connection with them. Rather than allowing your situation to put a strain on your relationship, let this season of uncertainty draw you closer to them. It's not a time of venting and complaining, but a time of praying and planning for the future. Speaking words of encouragement over your life and speaking a blessing over their lives for how they have handled things with you during your time of uncertainty speaks volumes. And God is glorified in it.

## It Takes G.R.I.T. to Press Through Your Situations

It takes grit to push through. Grit will move you forward when all you want to do is sit still. Grit will energize you when you feel weakened by your situation. Even with faith, you cannot escape the seasons of life that seek to weigh you down; but when you have grit, you don't have to stay down. Whatever struggles you are faced with, you should approach them with a GRIT attitude and determination to:

> **G**ive it your all
> **R**ealize God is with you
> **I**gnite your faith
> **T**rust God to get you through it

A few years ago, my husband surprised me with a bicycle for my birthday. I had been talking for some time about being more active and stepping up my exercise game by doing more than just walking for half an hour every other evening. I shared with him that not since my young adult days had I been on a bicycle, but I was interested in riding again. So, for my birthday, he showed up with a pearl white Schwinn bicycle, complete with the silver bell on the handlebar. He even got me a helmet, a water bottle and a small knapsack that I could store my granola bars in as I rode. I now had no excuse not to ramp up my exercise game.

That summer afternoon, we both put on our exercise clothes, filled our water bottles and got our bikes ready for a ride around our neighborhood. The first few minutes were exhilarating for me. I had moments of nostalgia thinking back to my younger years when I rode a red Schwinn bicycle with frequency and ease. My husband, an avid cyclist, had circled the neighborhood about four times as I barely made it from one end of our street to the other end. After a few minutes, I stopped pedaling and coasted my way back to our driveway. I had forgotten to shift gears as I was going up the slight incline on our street. My momentum was gone. My enthusiasm was gone, too. Because I had not ridden a bike in years, and I wasn't doing any kind of exercise other than walking, my muscles immediately felt the impact. I felt winded and my legs ached. I told my husband that considering these circumstances, it was very likely that I wouldn't be able to make it beyond our neighborhood.

I didn't have grit. I simply gave up. Instead of working my way through it, I threw in the towel. "In the context of behavior, grit is described as firmness of behavior, indomitable spirit...grit is more about attitude than an end game." It is about follow-through and having a sense of perseverance that motivates you even when you don't feel like doing anything. [1]

Sometimes that's what we do with our faith when things go wrong – we throw in the towel and give up. We don't shift our faith gears. Have you ever given up on something so quickly because things got rough? Have you ever been in a relationship that turned sour and the person you trusted ended up disappointing you and now you are determined not to trust anyone again? You might be facing one of the biggest challenges of your life and your friends have abandoned you. You might feel alone and scared, thinking that no one cares about your well-being. It can sound tempting to just wallow and stay where you are. As a believer, your faith in God is the first thing to get attacked when seasons of life hit. The devil wants you to believe that you are better off not trusting anyone, better off staying isolated and alienated, and better off giving up on God. But God wants you to know that you are never alone. God is always right there with you, no matter what. Grit is that inherent sense that, as a believer, you know without a doubt that you are in the grip of God's hand.

Sure, Naomi was salty with God and based on how her life had taken a wrong turn, she felt that God had dealt unkindly with her. She is not alone in that feeling. Certainly, there are believers, strong-minded Christians, who can become a little salty with God, but it does not diminish their faith in God. It is okay to be scared, anxious, unsettled and concerned about how your situation is impacting you, but don't throw in the towel on God. Naomi didn't throw in the towel. She expressed how she felt about her situation and she used it as motivation for elevation. She was in one of the worst places that a believer could live.

*God is always right there with you, no matter what.*

And it's in Moab of all places.

Sometimes life presents us with circumstances like this where we make choices that we think are the best and it ends up being the complete opposite. A few years ago, one of my good friends packed up her Ford Thunderbird and her pre-teen daughter, then left Dallas and moved to Chicago after experiencing a season of unexpected unemployment. She had been at the top of her game, working in the health field when suddenly the non-profit where she labored tirelessly began to lose its funding. The loss of funding meant loss of resources for its clients and ultimately loss of positions and salaries. What was once a fruitful and plentiful job had now become a place that could barely keep its doors open. After circulating her résumé and going to interview after interview, my friend was clear that Dallas no longer presented itself as a viable place for her and her young daughter. Add to that the frustration of being unemployed for seven months and nearing the end of her unemployment benefits (which is an oxymoron because there aren't many benefits to being unemployed), she went to Chicago on the promise of a job through a connection she had with a relative there.

A promise and the wing of a prayer. I made the trip with her, to help her drive and to be a presence of support. After she got settled in to Chi-town and into her new job, things seemed to be finally looking up for her, that is, until circumstances hit and situations beyond her control caused her to find herself unemployed – yet again – after only one year. The promise seemed to have turned to punishment, and the wing of a prayer that she rode on seemed to have been clipped.

She was empty and she questioned why would God do this to her and more so, she felt like God had turned against her. Plus, she had her thirteen-year-old daughter to consider. This impacted her, too. I'm sure that many of us, at one time or another, have felt this way. While we might never publicly acknowledge it because we don't want to be perceived as "Christians without faith," the reality is, we are all faith strugglers. The truth is that we all have had to deal with some circumstances and situations in life that have caught us off guard, caused us to question where God is, and it has left us empty, hoped out and frustrated.

That's what it must have been like for Naomi. She went from being the wife of this respected leader in Bethlehem to being his widow. We learn very quickly that she is in fact bitter. It's summed up in the first five verses of this narrative of this stage of her life. She and her husband, whose name means "My God is king," and their two sons, whose names unfortunately mean "perishing" and "disease," once lived in a land called Bethlehem, which means "bread of life," when a famine hits the land. And then a second blow happens. The unthinkable happens. Her husband, the patriarch of their family, dies. Yes, the one whose name means "My God is king." If that's not enough, life adds insult to injury some ten years later when both of her sons die. All that Naomi has left to hold onto is uncertainty and two daughters-in-law. Two Moabite women. Here they are, three women in a male-dominated society with no means and no man to care for them. Their livelihood was at risk and they were exposed. Naomi went from security to scarcity. I'm sure some of us would like to lean in and whisper to her: "The joy of the Lord is your strength," but Naomi is in a place of mistrust, hurt, brokenness and confusion.

Understandably, Naomi was bitter. She is like a lot of us who are in a season of brokenness and we feel the strain, the distance between hope and believing; the tension of trusting God but still having uncertainty about God's plan for our lives, and we are empty. There is this rushing wind of angst and anxiety swirling around in us, shaking our faith and rendering us to an uneasy sense of doubt. Empty. When will this season end? Empty like the air being squeezed out of you. Empty like running low on energy. Empty on patience and empty on hope. In this marathon of life where the race is not given to the swift or the strong, but to the one who endures, we wonder how much more of this we can endure. And it has caused us to become bitter, too.

Yes, Naomi was salty with God, but she still believed in God. Verse six of this text says, "Then she started to return with her daughters-in-law from the country of Moab, for she had heard in the country of Moab that the Lord had considered his people and given them food." Even after all this time in Moab, being subjected to the life there, the death of her husband and sons there, the loss of being able to openly practice her faith there, Naomi still considered herself a "people" of God. She was still willing to give God another chance. We know this is true because she based her decision to return to Bethlehem on the fact that God was once more providing for God's people. In other words, we can find ourselves in the throes of being hurt, being salty, and being disgruntled because things aren't going our way, and we're so far from what we planned, yet when we keep our ears and hearts open to the movement of God, we can be assured that God is going to move in our situation. This is a reminder that we must never give up on God because in this covenant relationship that we are in with the Great Almighty, God will never give up on us.

*We must never give up on God. God will never give up on us.*

It is also a reminder that we must stay in contact with people who will tell us what God is up to. The only way that Naomi knew what was happening back in Bethlehem is because people were talking about the goodness of God. It is during those times of spiritual famine where we feel like our faith is at its lowest, that we must not lose our connection with people of faith who will pour into us by telling us that God is at work. The season of bad times had come to an end in Bethlehem. God was restoring the land, and in turn, the people's hope and joy were also being restored.

How often do we squander our future because we are still holding on to disappointment from the past? A relationship that turned sour. A job that ended. An unfavorable outcome in a medical diagnosis for ourselves or a loved one. We ascribe our pain as God somehow imposing a punishment against us or turning God's back on us and it leaves us feeling depleted and bitter. What happens when the seeds that you planted seem to no longer be growing? The crop of investments, time on your job, and the sacrifice in your relationships, all seem to have dried up. In *agricultural* terms, your field has burned up. In *spiritual* terms, your faith is in a drought. It's hard for you to believe God again in this one area of your life. In *tell it like it is* terms, you are broke, busted and disgusted. You feel as though God has gone AWOL on you, leaving you spiritually thirsty. Your faith is under attack. Where you were once thriving and flourishing, you are now barely making it.

Just because Naomi was living in a land with people who didn't profess God as their sovereign Lord, it didn't mean that she had to give up her faith. Yes, she was displaced for what seemed like it could become a permanent situation, but Naomi had the gumption, grit and determination to press through her season of disappointment so that she could get to the provision that God had for her in her hometown of Bethlehem. When you are going through difficulties, it's important to remember to give it your all. Face your struggles with the kind of grit that will give you the determination in spite of the desperation of your situation. It is in times like this that you must rely on your faith and not get sidetracked by what you are experiencing. Matthew 17:20 records Jesus saying that if you have faith the size of a mustard seed, you can use that faith to move mountains and change your situation. If nothing else, faith will change your outlook on your situation. Faith will help you to see that God is with you and that God is for you. If you have accepted Jesus Christ as your Lord and Savior, then you are in a covenant relationship. Nothing can break that bond. You might not always step up and do your part in the relationship, but God will always do God's part. Think about how much more forcefully you can press through life's struggles when you approach them with grit. Facing your situations with an attitude of grit helps you produce a fearless kind of faith.

### Realize God is with You

An amazing turn of events in Naomi's faith journey happens when she tries to persuade her two daughters-in-law, Orpah and Ruth, to turn back and go to their mother's home. After some time of talking and then weeping, Orpah follows her mother-in-law's directives, but Ruth is determined to press through the struggle, and remain with Naomi. Ruth shows that she has grit. In fact, Ruth clings on to her mother-in-law. She does more than talk the talk. She demonstrates her faith in Naomi.

Wait a minute!

Here we have a young woman who grew up in Moab, a land where the people denounce God Almighty in favor of idols and a pagan god, and Ruth has the fortitude and foresight to show faith. Ruth watched her sister-in-law Orpah depart and head for home, but she insisted on staying with Naomi. The text records Ruth saying in verses 16 and 17, "Do not press me to leave you or to turn back from following you! Where you go, I will go; where you lodge, I will lodge; your people will be my people, and your God, my God. Where you die, I will die – there will I be buried. May the Lord do thus and so to me, and more as well, even if death parts me from you!"

So, let's back up a minute. Naomi is bitter with God. She openly expresses that God has dealt unkindly with her. She then offers a blessing in the form of encouraging words over her two daughters-in-law. She admonishes them to leave. And she says that they have a chance for a better life since they are still young. And once more she exclaims that "The hand of the Lord has turned against me." It is in the midst of this exchange of words and the pouring out of her soul that Naomi shares the lowest point of her faith, yet Ruth announces that she is willing for this same God – the one who dealt bitterly with Naomi – to be her God. Do you know that the way you handle your faith in your season of strife and disappointment can still be a moment of witnessing to someone else, and it can still bring someone else to want to know your God? Think about that for a moment. Naomi is still calling on the name of the Lord even though she feels hurt and disappointed. If you are in a season of life that is unsettling, disappointing and has you feeling some kind of way, are you still willing to call on the name of the Lord in spite of? Has God heard you utter God's name? Have you remembered that you are in a covenant relationship with the Creator of the Universe, and that no matter if you are feeling some kind of way, God is still sovereign and is still in a position to help you press through your situation? Are you ready to expose your situation to God Almighty? Even with a broken and contrite heart you can still turn to God. Do you realize that God wants you to turn your bitterness into fearless faith so that you can press your way through this struggle?

Ruth had some kind of grit! She could have easily left with Orpah and gone back to her mother's house, but she made a declaration to stay with Naomi.

Talk about a defining moment.

Ruth heard Naomi say that the Lord had turned the Lord's hand against her mother-in-law, yet she was still willing to take the Lord as her Lord, and to take the Lord's hand – a hand that would lead her into a future with hope and a promise. The great gospel songwriter, Thomas Dorsey, was also willing in spite of his tragic circumstances. He knew what it meant to call on the name of the Lord in the midst of a troubling season. In 1932, his wife died while giving birth to the couple's son. If that wasn't enough to deal with, Dorsey was hit with a second loss when their newborn son died just two days later. Dorsey could have easily turned away from God and become bitter, but it was out of this loss and grief that he wrote, *Precious Lord, Take My Hand*, one of the best-known songs in gospel history. Dorsey displayed the kind of strength and fearless faith that helped him to press through such a traumatic experience. When most people would have probably given up and turned inward, Dorsey demonstrated an amazing level of grit. I believe it is because Dorsey realized that God was with him. That experience, as devastating as it was, shaped the history of gospel music. If it had not been for Dorsey's grit, we wouldn't have this song of comfort in our time of need. If it had not been for his determination to press through this gut-wrenching experience, this song would have not become a signature piece in gospel legend Mahalia Jackson's repertoire. Out of his pain, Dorsey gave us a powerful song with purpose. Out of Dorsey's pain, God still led him to a life of promise. The song magnifies who the Lord is in our moments of weakness brought on by the trials of life.

It is a cry to God to hold our hand in the tough seasons of life, and to be assured that God will do it because of the covenant relationship that we are in. A covenant that will not waiver – even when our faith does.

It takes a whole lot of grit and fearless faith to press through life's struggles.

## Ignite Your Faith

Too often we shift too quickly to feeling defeated in our circumstances. What was supposed to be a temporary setback can easily become a prolonged step back if we confront it with the wrong mindset. Pressing through your struggles with fearless faith requires you to stop complaining and to start planning. For some of us, we see a setback and throw in the towel immediately. We sign a contract with the problem, make a down payment on it and settle in as if it's a three-year lease agreement – or worse, we sign the deed and take permanent ownership of the problem. Don't give your problems that kind of power. Instead, commit to praying and planning. Plan for the steps you need to make. Plan for the resources you need and then identify people or agencies that can assist you with getting them. Plan for the life you desire, the job you desire, the apartment or house that you desire, and then ignite your faith.

*Stop complaining and start planning.*

I can remember when I was little, we had the kind of stove that had a blue light to it. I didn't know it at the time, but that blue light is called a pilot light. When my mother got ready to cook, she had to make sure that the pilot light was lit. If it wasn't lit, she'd have to strike a match and ignite the coil so that the flame would rise up, creating that blue light. Our breakfast depended on it. Our dinner depended on it. And those sweet potato pies that my mother made during the holidays depended on it. If we didn't see the blue light, that meant that the stove would not work. It wasn't that something was wrong with it; it's that the flame had not been ignited. This didn't require calling for a service repair. It didn't require getting a new stove. The only thing that needed to happen was to ignite what was already there. The pilot light was waiting to be ignited. That's how it is with our faith. God is waiting for us to ignite our faith. The faith is already there. It might be flickering

*You must be intentional about having bold faith.*

at times like the pilot light. It might feel like it's not even on; but all it takes is a spark of belief that God, your pilot light, can and will do something about your situation. God is able. When God sees that you have even the tiniest spark, God will do God's part to make the flame of your faith shine bright. The enemy wants you to believe that the pilot light is out permanently. The enemy is hoping that your disappointments will douse your faith. The enemy is counting on your failed attempt to fuel your fear. The enemy wants you to give up. The enemy wants you to give up on God, but you must be intentional about having bold faith – fearless faith that says you will press your way through this season of life. Strike a match of hope. Strike a match of determination. Strike a match of belief and watch God take your little spark of faith and turn it into fearless faith.

In 1949, Esther McCready ignited her fearless faith and didn't give up. As a little girl growing up in segregated Baltimore, Maryland, she dreamed of being a nurse. She began pursuing that dream while she was a student at the all-black Dunbar High School. She worked as a nurse's aide at Sinai Hospital. It was only natural, then, that when she graduated high school, she applied to a nursing school program. McCready had a defining moment when she applied for admission to the University of Maryland School of Nursing. It was defining because no African Americans had ever been admitted to the nursing program. When she was denied admission, solely because of her race, this young woman pressed her way through the frustration and was determined to be a nursing student at the school. With grit and fearless faith, she didn't settle for attending school all the way in Tennessee at Meharry Medical College, where African American students were expected to get their medical training. She wanted to remain close to her family in Maryland and attend school where she could glean all that was needed to be a degreed, professional and successful nurse.[2]

She didn't let the failed attempt of applying for admission extinguish her dream. With the help of civil rights giants Thurgood Marshall, Charles Hamilton Houston and Donald Gaines Murray, this young woman sued and won the right to be admitted to the University of Maryland. One year after her initial application for admission, she became the first African American to be admitted, attend and graduate from the nursing school. She then passed her state board nursing exams and enjoyed a successful career as a nurse and teacher. While she waited for the court's decision, she kept her eye on what was most important. While she waited, she studied and developed a plan. While she waited, she kept her drive and determination ignited.

## Trust God to Get You Through It

Every once in a while, we need a "then" moment to motivate us to do something different. Naomi had a "then" moment. After she had experienced the death of her husband, the death of her two sons, and looked around at her situation, at where she was living, and thought about how she could not make ends meet, she knew she had to make a serious decision. She decided to leave from her situation. Her "then" moment was the first step that led to Naomi making a conscious decision to not let her situation consume her. What I find admirable about Naomi, is that even though she was uncertain of what the future might hold, she was certain that she didn't want her future to look like her present. She was certain that she didn't want to remain in this situation. She was certain that even as a woman living in an Israelite culture where women didn't have the means or the opportunities to support themselves, at the very least she could leave from where she was and go to where she had a chance at improving her life. Naomi's faith journey began anew in verse 6 where it is recorded: "then she started to return with her daughters-in-law from the country of Moab, for she had heard in the country of Moab that the Lord had considered his people and given them food." It came immediately after her reality of being left alone without male provision pushed her to rely on God's providential provision.

*What is my "then" moment?"*

As you read this, ask yourself: "what is my "then" moment?" What needs to happen for you to decide that you are ready to press through whatever struggle you are in, whatever circumstances have you distraught, and whatever problem is weighing you down? Once you identify what that is, your "then" moment will be the catalyst that causes you to step up with fearless faith and prepare yourself to make a change. The Rev. Dr. Martin Luther King, Jr. said "Faith is taking the first step even when you can't see the whole staircase."[3] Naomi didn't see the whole staircase. Ruth didn't see the whole staircase. But they were willing to at least decide that they didn't want to remain in the situation that they were in. They were willing to take a risk and trust God to get them through it. Ruth made a strong declaration of faith when she proclaimed that Naomi's God would be her God. She spoke these words out loud. Sometimes our fear needs to hear our faith. We need to speak out loud the words of faith that will conquer our fear.

*Silence your fears with the words of faith that you speak.*

Silence your fears with the words of faith that you speak. Drown out the volume of the negativity that the enemy plants in your head. Turn up the speakers so that your faith reverberates to every corner of your mind where doubt sits.

Let these words be the soundtrack to your life's struggles: *God, I declare that my faith will speak louder than my fears*. Say it again like you really mean it. And keep saying it until you have convinced yourself of it.

Too often, we think that we don't have options when the truth is we can either stay in the situation that we are in, or we can trust God to get us through it and on to something better. If you never even attempt to see where your fearless faith will take you then you will never fully know what God will do for you. Many times we

*God created us to be in community with one another.*

tell ourselves all the reasons something won't work. We begin to limit ourselves based on education, work experience, past mistakes, family problems, or finances. We don't give our faith a chance, but we do give our excuses a chance. Ruth was new in her faith. We can surmise that her conversion experience or her "come to Jesus" moment was when she declared that she would stay with Naomi. That Naomi's God would be her God. This is significant because we know that she grew up in a culture that didn't honor God. We can assume that she became a believer based on her relationship and connection to her mother-in-law, Naomi. The story doesn't provide much in the way of her background, but we do know that at some point Ruth was living in the house with her husband and her in-laws, people who were from the town of Bethlehem. Just being around people of faith will help to build up your faith. When things go wrong, it's easy to begin isolating and alienating yourself from people, and from the fellowship of the family of faith. If you are part of a Christian church community, let that relationship help to build your faith. If you have someone who can and is willing to be your accountability partner – a person who will encourage you to pray, read God's word and spend time in devotion, invite that person in to help build your faith. Your faith works best when you are in the company of other believers who are also actively engaged in their covenant relationship with God. God created us to be in community with one another to bear witness to each other's pain, to fellowship together and to break bread together. These are the kinds of relationships that you need, especially when you are trying to press your way through the struggles of life. If you are a student, look for small groups on campus where other students are engaged in studying God's word.

In some sense, Ruth was more persistent and determined than Naomi. Ruth demonstrated fearless faith. She was willing to leave her homeland of Moab, the only place that she had ever known, and follow Naomi in hopes of a better life. More than that, she was willing to trust God. Her faith is what enabled her to have a "no matter what" kind of attitude. No matter what happens, I'll go. The Lord can do thus and so to me, and I'll still go. Ruth was not afraid to speak her faith! Naomi tried unsuccessfully to persuade Ruth to go back home, but Ruth stepped up with fearless faith and committed to what was ahead of her, not what was behind her.

## The Beginning of the Comeback Ministry

Ruth and Naomi left Moab and headed to Bethlehem. This was one of the hardest things that the two of them would have to do. Two women. Alone. Traveling from one town to another. The text doesn't go into specifics of what that journey was like for them, but we can imagine that it wasn't easy. First, consider their mode of travel. There was no Uber, cab, or public transportation. Second, they had to consider which belongings they could afford to take on this nearly 50-mile (doubled or tripled, depending on which route they took) trek from Moab to Bethlehem. They had to limit their load so that it would not weigh them down. They also had to consider how many days it would take for their journey. Fifty miles doubled or tripled is a long way to travel by foot or by animal. The physical endurance alone was enough to contend with, yet they were willing to push beyond all the barriers in order to get to Bethlehem. Though Naomi had traveled this road before, it had been more than ten years since she made the trek, and she made it with her husband and two sons. She was head-ing into Moab at that time. She had protec-tion, provision and her provider. Now she is heading out of Moab, out of her Moab ex-perience, and into Bethlehem. She is press-ing her way, and she has her young daughter-in-law with her who has only known the city limits and surroundings of Moab all her life.

*God will transition your trials into testimonies of victorious praise.*

This was going to be some transformational journey – for both of them!

When they finally made it to Bethlehem, they were imme-diately greeted by the women of the town. The women were surprised to see Naomi. The whole town was stirred because of them. In this context, the word "stirred" means that the towns-people were perplexed or confused by Naomi's and Ruth's ar-rival. It was followed by an impartial question of not just seek-ing whether or not this is Naomi, but more so, the expressive shock perhaps that she has survived her situation and is back in town. "Is this Naomi?" It can easily be viewed as a loaded question or as one of concern. Naomi's appearance and coun-tenance was certainly the talk of the town and it caused quite a stir. Don't be surprised that when God begins to turn things around for you, there will be some people who are perplexed and confused by your comeback ministry. They won't under-stand how you pressed through your struggles with fearless faith. They won't acknowledge your grit and determination. They might even start to raise rumors rather than celebrate your comeback. But don't get caught up in their issues and in-securities. Get caught up in the comeback that you are making and the God who is making it possible. God will do something transformative with those years of hardship. God will transi-tion your trials into testimonies of victorious praise.

Naomi was making a comeback.

A lot had changed in the ten years or more since Naomi left her homeland. She had changed. This woman who left as a wife and mother, now returned as a childless widow. The hardships had taken their toll on her, so much so that her first words to the women when they inquired if this was Naomi, were: "Call me no longer Naomi, call me Mara, for the Almighty has dealt bitterly with me. I went away full but the Lord has brought me back empty; why call me Naomi when the Lord has dealt harshly with me, and the Almighty has brought calamity upon me?"

That's some true transparency. I like to think of this as one of those moments where the woman is surrounded by a cir- *Her feelings are real and raw.* cle of her girlfriends and they are assessing this sister's situation as they hear from the most true and deepest place of her pain. Naomi was being one hundred percent real about her experience. "MiMi" kept it real. She went to that deep place that is in so many of us where it's like our pain rises, takes voice, and says what we aren't courageous enough to say.

Well, that's a lot coming from a woman whose name means "sweet," or "pleasant." Interestingly her life was a stark contrast to the essence of who she was. There was nothing pleasant about being out of fellowship with the faith community for ten years or more. There was nothing sweet about losing the love of her life and her two sons. These words that she spoke are about as raw and real as a Taylor Swift rift or a soundtrack featuring Beyoncé, Carrie Underwood, Mary J. Blige or a Miranda Lambert belly-aching song except that the person that MiMi is talking about is God. Creator of the Universe. The one who breathed life into Adam and fashioned woman, Eve, from his rib. Yeah. That's who has MiMi feeling some kind of way. Her feelings are real and raw. This was grief talking. It was the gut-wrenching pain and angst and heartache of a woman who saw her whole life fall apart, and now here she was, at this age, trying to start over again. Sometimes "again" is "a gain." You gain grit. You gain experience. You gain perspective.

Has your narrative ever looked like that? Have you ever been vulnerable and transparent enough with God to tell God how you really feel about your situation? I believe that it is helpful to get it all out so that you can empty yourself of those feelings that have manifested deep inside your heart and soul. It's spiritual cleansing. It will free you up for the journey that is before you. As you get ready to lace up your spiritual walking shoes and mentally prepare yourself to get out of your Moab situation, you will need all the energy and strength you can muster up, especially if you've been stagnant for a while.

I remember being part of the Girl Scouts Troop when I was younger. I started at the level called Brownie when I was in second grade. It taught me some life lessons on building friendships, interacting with people as I sold those yummy cookies, and it taught me something else I had never done in my seven years of living: how to go hiking. Hiking and exploring the outdoors was a major part of the Girl Scouts program. I still remember when our troop leader took us hiking at Kiest Park in Dallas. It was scary for me because I didn't have any experience or training in walking a distance other than being on the sidewalk playing Simon Says with my friends. Hiking taught me to rely on the other people who were on this journey with me. It taught me to trust my instincts and to keep pressing through the weeds, tall grass, and annoying bugs on the trail. I had to learn how to focus, and to look for a clearing while swatting bugs and pushing past swinging branches that blocked the trail. As a seven-year-old, I felt overwhelmed at what looked like I was navigating through a forest when in reality, our trail was just leading us from one side of the park to the other side. We weren't as isolated as it seemed. We still heard the cars in the distance driving by. Even though I didn't know where the path would lead to, I knew that our troop leader knew. She was responsible for guiding us through the forest and to our destination. There is no way that I could have done it alone.

In hindsight, I realize that those simple walks along the sidewalk provided the training that I needed for our troop hikes. You must train and be able to maintain a level of endurance for the journey. It's the same way with your faith. You have to do some faith training along the way – prayer walks, spiritual exercises, and devotions. These exercises

*Trust God to get you through it.*

will give you the energy for the journey ahead, especially in those times when you want to give up and turn back. If you want your faith life to be strong, you have to work at it. Relying on God, your "troop leader" is extremely important, but you have to do your part to make sure you are able to press through your struggles with endurance. If you give up at the first sight of annoying bugs that come your way, you will never make it out of your spiritual famine. If you allow the swinging branches along the path to distract you and to dissuade you from going on, you will end up right back where you already were – a place that is no longer healthy for your well-being. Trust God to get you through it. God is the only

*Don't fall for the enemy's tactics.*

one who can see what's ahead and down the path where God is leading you. Yes, you can be facing some uncertainty; but when you pray for clarity, God will make God's will known. Yes, there will be distractions along the way, but God will help to keep you focused. The psalmist writes in Psalm 141:9, "Keep me safe from the traps set by evildoers, from the snares they have laid for me." [4] The enemy will set traps along the way to discourage you. The enemy will place snares in your path to make you turn back. Don't fall for the enemy's tactics. Instead, hold on to God's unchanging hand – a hand that will not let you fall or falter.

And here's a sure sign that you are pressing through with fearless faith: your "walking" shoes will show all the signs of wear and tear from the journey. If there are no scuffs (trials) or smudges (setbacks), then you haven't really begun to walk. People and situations will test you. The enemy will test you. God will test you. The difference is that God will never send you through any situation without the covering of mercy and grace. God will not send you on a path to fail. You should also expect some gravel and rocks to get underneath your foot, to irritate you to the point that you have to take off your shoes and shake away the disturbance. Dare I say that there will be some "grit" in your shoes. Let this grit be a reminder that you are in training for the journey that is ahead. You can still make it because God is with you every step of the way.

*God will not send you on a path to fail.*

# Be Fearless

## REFLECTION QUESTIONS

God knows you might be salty about some things. God wants you to have GRIT: *Give it your all; Realize God is with you; Ignite your faith; Trust God to get you through it;*

**What situation or disappointment are you salty with God about?**

_____

_____

_____

_____

_____

**List one action step that you are willing to take to turn your saltiness into grit (speak faith over your fear, ask someone to pray with you, join a small group, etc.)**

_____

_____

_____

# CHAPTER THREE

# A Season of Hurt Produces a Season of Harvest

*"So she went. She came and gleaned in the field behind the reapers. As it happened, she came to the part of the field belonging to Boaz, who was of the family of Elimelech."*
— Ruth 2:3 —

My husband and I have an area in our living room that is designated "plant city." I have ivies whose arms outstretch and encircle our sofa table, sprawl along the wall and then some. One of these ivies belonged to my mother. She planted it all the way back in 1980 and it is still growing and multiplying! In fact, the other ivies that I have are the "offspring" of this 37-year-old plant. It might sound impossible, but when you begin to understand the power of planting seeds, watering and nourishing the seeds, and exposing them to the right amount of light, you will see that the seeds you planted some thirty plus years ago, will continue to provide a harvest for the next generation. That plant has endured climate change, days that were unseasonably hot and nights that were unseasonably cold. It has survived moving from our family house, to my mother's senior living residence, to now residing in my home.

Through the journey, though, it continued to thrive. Each of my siblings has been gifted with plants from that three-decades-old ivy. My niece is now part of that "ivy" heritage. My mother took one of the "arms" of the ivy about five years ago and "planted" an ivy for her. It, too, is sprawling, healthy and green. And to this day, we are seeing the increase of what my mother planted 37 years ago! Yes, there are a few times when the plant looked puny, had lots of dead leaves that needed to be snipped, and soil that was dry and crackling, but the love, work and care that my mother put into planting that ivy is what causes it to still be standing.

*The seeds of faith that you plant today will multiply and produce a great harvest.*

God's Word reminds us of the new life that is planted through seeds provided by God. Apostle Paul writes in 2 Corinthians 9:10: *He who supplies seed to the sower and bread for food will supply and multiply your seed for sowing and increase the harvest of your righteousness."*

What seeds are you planting – even in your season of bitterness, hurt and disappointment? The seeds of faith that you plant today will multiply and produce a great harvest. In order to press through the struggles of life, you need the kind of faith that can endure the unseasonable changes that bring about frustration, discontent and hard times. You need the kind of faith, that in times when it looks puny and frail, it can still survive because of the love, work and care that you put into watering and nourishing your faith. This faith is the fearless kind that is able to withstand the climate changes of life and it will get you through those moments of what feels like spiritual famine, and carry you to your harvest.

Naomi went through a lot of climate changes – spiritual climate changes. When we are introduced to her situation, we see that her story begins with her family being in Bethlehem. As noted earlier, Bethlehem means "bread of life." Naomi's husband Elimelech was from an upper crust family, yet the famine that hit their hometown was so great that they had to be displaced and move to Moab. Moab was booming and thriving with food yet it was spiritually dry. In essence, Naomi went through two famines: a physical famine in Bethlehem, where there was no longer any food for nourishment, and then a spiritual famine in Moab because there was no feeding of God's word. Even in her declaration that God had turned against her, Naomi still had a seed of faith that sustained her through the tough times. If she didn't, there is no way that she would have been willing to press through her angst and agony to return to Bethlehem. The seed of faith that was planted and nourished in Bethlehem is what carried Naomi through her Moab season of famine.

After a very long and trying season of hurt, Naomi's harvest was coming. Like any of us would do, she lamented her situation, cried out in defeat to God, rehearsed her bitterness to her daughters-in-law and felt the weight of the world upon her. Yet, she still had a defining moment where, in the midst of her pain, she pushed through and made a declaration that she would return to Bethlehem. She didn't know what she was returning to or what the conditions were, yet she knew that the risk was worth it. And it was definitely worth it. At the end of chapter 1, the last words are: "They came to Bethlehem at the beginning of the barley harvest." God came through for Naomi and Ruth! There is no way they could have known what they were walking into. They had no idea how long their "faith" walk from Moab to Bethlehem would take, but God knew. And God honored their faith and risk by allowing their return to coincide with the beginning of the barley harvest season.

Talk about divine timing!


**Timing Is Everything**

Trust God even when you are uncertain about what's ahead and you can't trace where God is. Believe, though, that God is always present. God is either in the middle of it with you, on the periphery guiding you or many steps ahead of you, clearing the way.

*God is either in the middle of it with you, or many steps ahead of you.*

I recognize that it's hard to see with our natural eyes that destiny is on the other side of disaster. When you've been in a situation for so long, it's much easier to see life through the gaping holes of doubt than it is to see through the frames of faith. When you've been in a season of hurt, disappointment, and barely making it, your reality quickly sets in. In these seasons, it is also very likely that your faith has lost its zest. The spiritual dial on your faith has moved from enthusiastic and robust to tepid and without passion.

Recently, I was shopping for some household items and I ended up on the aisle that displays crock pots. They come in different sizes. The smaller versions are used for cooking foods like nachos and chili, and the larger ones are used for slow cooking roasts and stews. My husband and I have a larger one that I use when I cook his favorite meal – beef pot roast. What I like about the crock pot is that it has three settings: warm, low and high. Depending on how long you want the meal to cook, you can set the dial for your desired cooking time. I usually prepare our meal, place it on low, and head to work with the expectation that over the span of seven or eight hours, it will cook slowly. Other times, when I've gotten a late start, I will set the dial for high, and the roast will be ready in about four hours. Sometimes we treat faith that same way. We want to set the dial based on how long we are willing to wait on God to change our situation. And when the timing doesn't coincide with our timetable, we easily become anxious, bitter and we can feel that God's hand is turning against us. We get upset and throw in the towel, not realizing that we are so close to getting to our season of harvest. We get that sinking feeling, we lose faith, and fear sets in. We also tend to forget that God is right there with us. Joshua 1:9 encourages us to stay the course and to remain hopeful in spite of what's happening. "I hereby command you: Be strong and courageous; do not be frightened or dismayed, for the Lord your God is with you wherever you go."

## Cultivating Blessings

Ruth and Naomi walked into their harvest.

Not just metaphorically.

They actually *walked* to their season of harvest.

And it took a lot of walking and determination to get there. Before we skip past the journey that it took for them to make it to Bethlehem, let's think about what that walk could have been like for these two women, traveling alone. Traveling any distance would have been risky and out of the ordinary for two women. Walking from one town to another was no doubt risky. Without knowing all the particulars about the route that they took, or the length of time that it took, we can surmise a few things. One, we know that it is approximately 40 to 50 miles between Moab and Bethlehem. We also know that because of the terrain, it is highly unlikely that this was a direct route, meaning that they had to make their away around the Dead Sea. This wasn't a straight-line shot. Two, we know that it is next to impossible to make this trip in just a few days. In fact, it is likely that it took them anywhere from five to seven days to make this trip, crossing the Jordan River and walking a hilly path to get to their destination. Moab was situated just near the Dead Sea and the Jordan River. Moab was also a country with lots of hills. It is safe to say that Ruth and Naomi's journey was mostly uphill.

Life is like that sometimes.

There will be hills to climb along this faith journey that we must endure so that we can get to the destination that God has for us. We all have our rivers to cross. There is no avoiding it. Before you can celebrate walking into your Bethlehem experience, you have to make it through the muck and mire of your Moab situation. In other words, your mountaintop experience requires you to climb the mountain.

*Your mountaintop experience requires you to climb the mountain.*

Do you know that even now God is mapping out your route to help you get out of your Moab situation and into your Bethlehem season of harvest?

We can also assume that part of their journey took place during the darkness of the night, meaning that Naomi and Ruth had to camp out somewhere when nightfall hit. So, here you have the two of them, already experiencing some dark moments in their lives, and now they are walking to their season of harvest amid the darkness of night. Perhaps they set out at dawn, traveling as far as they could, for as long as they could, but at some point, they needed to stop and rest. The mental and physical toll that this trip was taking meant that they had to endure the dark moments. And let's not forget the heaviness of the season that they were walking *out of*, walking *through* and walking *in* to get to their harvest. They were two women grieving.

Walking with the burden of loss.

Walking as two widows.

Walking with the uncertainty of what they'd find in Bethlehem, but knowing for sure that the God of Israel was there.

That, they could be certain of!

There's a lot that we don't know about the small details because it is not shared; yet we know enough to recognize that it was a dark moment. At some point in time, we all have to endure the dark moments. Just like in this story of Ruth, not every one of our experiences is recorded on paper either. Never the less, it doesn't mean that the experience didn't happen or that it didn't have a profound affect.

Naomi and Ruth, forever linked by their loss, their grit and their willingness to keep pressing, didn't let the stretch of road that was ahead of them discourage them from going on.

And that's important. It's important because many times we get stuck in where we are because we start looking at the obstacles that we might face rather than the opportunity that we will have. We lose sight of the promise because we focus on the possibility of problems.

Be encouraged and know that the same God who met Naomi and Ruth in Bethlehem is the same God who is with you right now and will meet you in your season of harvest.

*We get stuck in where we are because we start looking at the obstacles.*

And that's important.

The timing of their decision to leave from Moab couldn't have been more impeccable. I don't think that it was coincidence; rather, I believe it was God's timing and providence. When you are walking in faith, relying on God and trusting God for the provision, things will line up according to God's plan – even when it doesn't make sense in the natural thinking. Faith is not about doing things in the natural. It is about following God and yielding to the supernatural! When we take the steps to follow God, God will lay out the rest of the steps for us. And those steps will lead to some extraordinary and amazing experiences.

*Take the steps to follow God.*

As soon as Ruth and Naomi arrived in Bethlehem, Ruth didn't waste any time stepping into the opportunity that was before her. She observed other people gleaning in the fields. She didn't judge the people who were there. She didn't think too highly of herself that this was too much or to belittling for her to do. No, Ruth seized the opportunity that God had placed before her. Too often, we don't step into the opportunities that God provides for us. We analyze it instead of aligning ourselves with it. We gripe about how it looks instead of being grateful. Sometimes we are too ornery and prideful to do the work because we somehow think it diminishes our worth. God will never undermine your worth. God created you! Psalm 139 expresses our worth through God's eyes and it is our motivation to press through. "I praise you for I am fearfully and wonderfully made. Wonderful are your works; that I know very well." [5] If God's work is wonderful then doesn't it stand to reason that the work God sets before us is wonderful, too?

Ruth took initiative and showed grit. She asked her mother-in-law for permission to go to the fields and glean among the ears of grain. If you look closer at the verse and at what she was asking, Ruth was seeking permission with a very specific purpose and goal in mind. Verse 2 says, "Let me go into the field and glean among the ears of grain, behind someone in whose sight I may find favor." Did you catch the purpose of her request? *Behind someone in whose sight I may find favor*? Let's pause there for a moment. Ruth is a newcomer to faith. Yet she does what many of us do not do: she is intentional and purposeful in her request. Though she was asking this of Naomi, this same kind of grit and fearless faith is needed when we are praying to God. Don't be afraid to be specific in your prayer to God. The more time you spend with God, the more your prayers will align with God's purpose for you. Your prayer life will begin to shift. Your focus will move from struggling to pray to standing firm in prayer.

God honored Ruth's request of Naomi. Of all the fields and areas of the fields that Ruth could have gleaned in, she ended up in the part of the field that belonged to a man named Boaz, whom we soon discover is part of Elimelech's family. God was on the scene, and had gone ahead of Ruth and secured the place where her feet would tread. All she had to do was allow her steps to be ordered by God. She took a risk by leaving Moab. She was willing for Naomi's God to be her God, and she exuded the kind of fearless faith that led her to have the courage to go to the fields and work. Just imagine what God will provide for you when you take a risk on God!

Ruth's future was being cultivated by the workers in the field. She reaped the blessing because she was willing to do something different. Back in Moab, it's very likely that she had never experienced working outside of the home before. Culturally, women worked inside the home, attending to their husband and children. As a young married woman, Ruth likely never did any toiling of the land. But as a widow, she had to open herself to doing something different. Her livelihood depended on it. Her comfort zone was gone. She was in Bethlehem determined to make a new start for herself and for her mother-in-law.

When God sees our willingness, there are times when the inexplicable happens and we reap the benefits of our fearless faith. Right now, I believe that God is cultivating your future. God is on the scene, working out your "tomorrow" this very moment. All you need to do is step out on faith and trust that the work is worth it. When we are unafraid to walk on the holy ground that God is preparing for us, and allow our steps to be ordered by the Lord, the Creator of the Universe will produce fruit on the places where our feet tread. In the same way that God was cultivating provision and a provider for Ruth, God will do it for us. Your provider might be a new job opportunity, a second stream of income, a financially supportive spouse or a return on an investment. If we choose instead to stay right where we are and let the grass grow under our feet, then we forfeit the blessing that is waiting for us. You will never see the harvest that God has for you if you don't trust God enough, and see your future through God's eyes. Maybe you've been pressing through life a long time, trying to push your way through the struggles of abandonment, hurt, financial woes, insecurity in your relationship, an unfinished college degree, a goal that you keep starting and stopping. Perhaps you've made some significant progress, but find yourself getting tired and weary. There's also a possibility that your prayer life has waned, your enthusiasm for studying and applying God's word is lukewarm and your harvest feels so far away. Even if these things are true, you have to keep pressing.

Let me draw the picture to help you see it. In 1946, S. Truett Cathy and his brother, Ben, opened the Dwarf Grill in a suburb of Atlanta. Their first day's sales were a measly $58.20. That's less than $30 a piece! These brothers could have easily looked at that number and given up right then and there. But they pressed on. They kept working at it because they knew their worth was way more than sixty dollars. God honored their sacrifice and risk. Four years later, they opened their second location. Their biggest breakthrough came in 1961 when they invented the boneless breast of chicken sandwich and called it Chick-fil-A. They kept pressing. Six years later, Truett pioneered the concept of the "mall food court" when this eatery became the first fast food restaurant to be inside of a mall. Today Chick-fil-A does more than $2 billion in annual sales – all because these two brothers kept pressing.

When you keep pressing with fearless faith, God will order your steps and orchestrate things in such a way that you will be connected with the right people, the right opportunities and the right provisions. Ruth asked for favor and she found it. She found it first with God and secondly with Boaz. Boaz made an inquiry about Ruth and wanted to know who she was. Instead of going directly to Ruth, Boaz asked the person who was in charge of the reapers. He answered by identifying her by her status rather than by her name. In one quick reply, he informed Boaz that Ruth was a Moabite, that she came to Bethlehem with Naomi, and that she was from the country of Moab. In some sense, we could read his reasoning for saying this, thinking that he tried to highlight her past, seemingly hoping it would prevent her from being able to glean; that's one possibility. It was customary to identify a person by their familial status and connection. When you think about it, we still do that today. We refer to someone as "the daughter of," or "the son of," especially if they belong to a prominent family. A person's given name is not nearly as important as their family name and their roots.

Because God was on the scene, Ruth's past didn't matter. She could have been dismissed and removed from the fields simply because she was from the country of Moab, where they were known to worship gods instead of the One true sovereign God. Yet, God's provision and promise for Ruth's future was greater than her past. Yes, it's true that the biblical Levitical law allowed for widows, the poor and the indigent to collect whatever was remaining on the threshing floor after the grain had been gathered.[6] And the inquiry of who Ruth was led to the discovery that she wasn't just some random young woman out there hustling for food; she was connected to Elimelech's family, immediately elevating her and giving her some status and identification. And because of that, Ruth was able to enjoy the promise of the "leftovers" in the field. God provided. Ruth didn't quite know what to expect but she did walk boldly to the field believing that she would not leave empty-handed.

## Finding Favor in Your Field

*There is fruit on your field*

There is fruit on your field – you just have to be willing to work and then watch the fruits of your labor grow. When I was little, our Saturday morning routine consisted of going to Lone Star Donuts in Oak Cliff and then heading over to the Dallas Farmers' Market to buy fresh produce. It was a sight to see as a little kid. All those trucks backed up, under the pavilion, with loads and loads of just-picked fruit like apples, strawberries and peaches and crisp fresh vegetables such as beans, corn, squash and potatoes with the dirt still on them. These goods represented the harvest of the fields that each farmer owned. Most were from small country towns as far away as Gilmer in East Texas or as close as Watauga on the west side of Dallas. They owned land. They tilled the soil. They planted the seeds. And they worked their fields. I'm sure there were some days when it seemed like nothing was growing, and then overnight, beans started budding and sprouts started springing up. And it was enough to feed their families and to sell the rest, and make an honest living.

My mother loved supporting the farmers and she loved their harvest, because in her words, "There is nothing better than fresh fruits and vegetables, planted with love and picked by hand." For years, this was our routine every Saturday morning. My mother befriended many of the farmers and they'd sometimes have a special bushel of her favorite plums or juicy ripe cantaloupes waiting for her – at no extra charge. It's because she had established a relationship with them; they knew each other by name. And she knew that there was little chance of finding bruised fruit. Through the years, we watched as the farmers' children learned the business and shared in the weekend selling of their harvest. The fruits of their labor were growing. They were cultivating blessings that their children and the next generations could enjoy.

What about you? What are you cultivating in the field that God has given to you? Are you developing a business plan for that "side hustle" that you've been dreaming about turning into a full-time, profitable job? Do you take advantage of free networking opportunities in your area to meet and connect with the people who will allow you to come and "glean knowledge from their field?"

Have you started cultivating the blessing for the provision of that acceptance letter to that training program, nursing school, MBA program, or certification program? Have you submitted the financial aid form as a response to God that you are willing to work the field?

What organizations or agencies do you need to join in order to have the opportunity to plant new seeds and get fresh fertilization for your dreams? There is a season of harvest with your name on it. You have to be willing to do the work that is required of you to cultivate it, and tend to it, and care for it. And when you do, God will grant favor.

Being Ruth wasn't easy for a young Moabite woman in her new digs of Bethlehem, but she approached it with grit, grace and a fierce determination to secure her future – a future that God had already planted, purposed and provided for her.

She just had to get there. To leave from her Moab situation and get to the blessing in Bethlehem. Being "you" right now might not be easy, but if you believe and trust that God has already planted, purposed and provided a future for you, and if you are not afraid to walk in it, then you will not only see the fruits of your labor, but you will also bless the next generation. Even if you don't have children of your own, you can still bless the next generation by how you handle the field that God has given you. For those who will come after you, your field can be a source of blessing for them.

# Be Fearless
## REFLECTION QUESTIONS

When it comes to your life goals, professional goals or career goals, what field do you want to glean in?

_____

_____

_____

_____

_____

There might be some missed opportunities that you have overlooked because you didn't think you could glean anything from a particular field. Pray and ask God to show you what fields you might be overlooking and ask God to help you find favor in the sight of the right person. Write your responses here:

_____

_____

_____

_____

_____

_____

_____

# CHAPTER FOUR

# Finding Favor In His Sight

*"Then she fell prostrate, with her face to the ground, and said to him, "Why have I found favor in your sight, that you should take notice of me, when I am a foreigner?"*
*— Ruth 2:10 —*

Ruth spoke these words to Boaz in chapter two. God had provided for her in a major way and was protecting her, along with fulfilling the providential plan for her – and for us.

Yes, for us, too. God always blesses us so that we can be a blessing to someone else. And being Ruth – this new creature in Christ, in Bethlehem, blessed generations and generations after her. We'll get to that a little later.

We never quite know what God is up to or how our situation will turn into something so amazing that it blesses generations to come. When we are willing vessels for God, the Lord will do extraordinary things through us and for us. It's true right here in this scene on the field. Things are beginning to unfold. Ruth's future is about to be secured. And she doesn't even know it. Little did Ruth know that the Sovereign God of

*The Lord will do extraordinary things through us and for us.*

Israel had already set things in motion in the field belonging to Boaz. It wasn't by accident or chance that she gleaned that very day, in that very field. It was all part of God's plan. Deuteronomy 31:8 assures us that: "It is the Lord that goes before you. He will be with you; he will not fail you or forsake you. Do not fear or be dismayed."

As the readers of the second chapter of Ruth, we quickly discover that there is a man by the name of Boaz who is prominent, who is rich and who is a relative of Naomi. In fact, Boaz is described as a kinsman on her husband's side.

Things are already starting to look up for Naomi and Ruth.

And they've only been in Bethlehem a few days.

A few days. Already finding favor. The God of Israel had already divinely orchestrated this meeting. It was not happenstance or chance. It was part of God's divine plan, a plan that could only be set into action by Naomi and Ruth pressing their way through their struggles to get out of Moab and into Bethlehem. Without grit, they wouldn't have gotten to Bethlehem. Without fearless faith, they would have stayed stuck in their Moab situation and never gotten to Boaz who was there and ready to provide them with the physical food that they needed.

Think about what this means. For ten years or more, Naomi had been spiritually starved, barely holding on in a place where the God of Israel was not recognized and worshiped. She didn't have anyone to pour into her, to speak life over her situation. There were no devotionals, no morning prayer lines, no girls' night out of venting and encouraging each other. Nobody to speak to this sister's situation. Ruth was spiritually starved, too, because until she made a faith decision, at the critical moment that Naomi was leaving Moab, she did not know the God of Israel at all. And now, their spiritual and physical needs were being satisfied.

In Bethlehem – the town whose name means bread of life.

They were getting their lives back. For Ruth, it was the beginning of a new life. For Naomi, it was life restored.

Let's take some time to really explore how being Ruth meant that was she living into this new life of being a worshiper, of being a woman of God. It's easy to rush past the significance of her posture, position, her choice of words and her attitude, and run right to the end of the story. If we rush, then we miss the lessons of how we can incorporate some of her fearless faith into our situation. It is also important to examine her life

> *Being Ruth is very much about strength.*

through the lens of the times *then* and not through our modern lens of where we are in the twenty-first century. Some of what she does can easily be mistaken for weakness, for not being independent, for not being a strong woman, but I want to offer to you that being Ruth is very much about strength – a formidable strength of character, of grace, of grit and determination.

The posture that Ruth took while in the field was one of worship. How do we know? Because in verse 10 it says: "Then she fell prostrate, with her face to the ground." That is a position and posture of worship. Here she is, being Ruth – a new creature in the faith – and already she is adopting a practice of worship. Now before you make assumptions about whether it takes all that, falling prostrate with your face to the ground is the real, authentic definition of worship. The Hebrew (the original language that the Old Testament was written in) word for worship is *'sagad'* and it means to "fall down" or "prostrate oneself."

Back *then* in biblical times, and *now*, in these times. It's the biblical definition of worship.

Authentic worship is coming before the Lord in a posture of humility and bowing down before God. Prostrate means extending your arms out in a manner of reverence for who God is. Having your face to the ground symbolizes that God is so holy that one cannot look God directly in the face. This dates back to the time of the story of Moses in Exodus, when God summoned the prophet to the mountain, but told him in very certain terms that he would not be allowed to see God's face. [7]

There is nothing wrong with worshiping God through song, liturgical dance, hand-clapping and swaying back and forth. Nothing at all. Yet if you want to experience authentic worship, then it's bowing down in the presence of God whether that is at church or at home in your private time. Ruth modeled what it meant to worship. Now, keep in mind that at this moment, Ruth did not fully know who Boaz was. She didn't know if he was a man of royalty, a king, a priest or one of the judges who ruled the land. She just knew that he was someone with whom she found favor. In the dialogue exchange, Ruth heard words like "The Lord be with you," and "The Lord bless you." As the reader of this text, we know that his name is Boaz, but within the story, it is not yet revealed who he is. So even in verse 8 when Boaz greets Ruth with "Now listen my daughter," a term of endearment, friendliness, and protection, she still has no idea who he is. Being Ruth in this environment is new to her. The text doesn't give us a lot of specifics about what was happening on the field, or any peek into what others might have been doing when Boaz came to the field, but it is likely that Ruth responded the way that she did because she understood Boaz to be someone in authority when he began asking questions. As Boaz continues talking, Ruth learns that this man has authority over the field.

Now, she knows he owns the field. Now, she knows he is in charge. Now, she knows he is the decision-maker. In a time when patriarchy ruled the day, Ruth knew enough to show reverence and honor to Boaz because of his status, and more so, because of her status as a foreigner and as a woman. She was living in a society where positions of authority were held mostly by men, or patriarchs. And she understood that her identification as a woman and as a Moabite, in this narrative, placed her in a position of vulnerability.

Remember, we are reading this through the lens of *that* day, in *that* biblical time, in *that* biblical culture, not through the lens of women's rights and equality.

Besides, Ruth was new to this town, and she was a newbie in the faith. Her focus was on securing her future so that she would not live a marginalized life as a widow. She pressed through and showed initiative. She showed that she was willing to work alongside everyone else in that field so that she could glean and have food at the end of the day. Without a husband as provider, and no children, specifically sons, who could rise to the occasion, Ruth had no other way.

*She pressed through and showed initiative.*

The lesson here is this: when was the last time that you worshiped God in this way? I mean, really laid prostrate and bowed down in God's presence? I remember leading our congregation through this authentic act of worship one Sunday morning at St. Luke "Community" United Methodist Church in the middle of my sermon. Amid the perplexed looks, some members actually got out of their seats, made their way to the floor and kneeled as an expression of worship. Others made their way to the altar and bowed down with their faces turned toward the ground. And I moved from the pulpit to the floor and joined them.

*When was the last time that you worshiped God in this way?*

Now that was transformational! It was worship at a different level – albeit challenging – but at a level that demonstrated a sincere reverence for who God is as the Creator of the Universe, as the sustainer of you and me, as the One who continues to make a way out of no way.

I don't know if you've ever been there before, where you've needed God to make a way out of no way, and God did. To recall that experience during your time of worship makes it a lot easier to fall prostrate. It's a bold move. It's a show of fearless faith. It honors God and it begins to change your perspective and outlook. It gives you grit. It gives you gumption. This kind of authentic worship changes you.

And it begins to change your situation.

## An Attitude and Posture of Humility

Are you willing to worship God in such a radical "it doesn't take all of that" kind of way? If it moves the needle a little bit to get you out of the mental, physical and psychological place of your Moab experience, will you do it? Here's a thought: if a situation can cause us to fall to our knees in despair, then what's so hard about willingly falling to our knees to worship God in this authentic and real way?

I'll let you decide when and where you feel comfortable enough to try it. I'll be praying for you.

The next thing that is apparent in how Ruth approached the situation is her attitude of humility. She acknowledged

*God will exalt you.*

that she had found favor, yet she asked why. Being Ruth in this new setting came with learning about what it means to be a woman of God, a child of God, and she honored that with her posture and attitude of humility. Some of us might find it challenging and difficult to have humility when we've been in one hardship after another. Earlier we talked about how hardships will help you to hold on and develop a healthy prayer life. The same is true about being humble. James 4:10 declares: "Humble yourselves before the Lord and he will exalt you." Exalt here means that God will lift you up, lift you out of your situation, lift you out of that lack luster mindset, lift you out of despair and into your season of harvest.

*God can do all things and do them well.*

God will exalt you. God will do this when you humble yourself before the Holy One. In the Greek text of this word "exalt" in this passage of James, the word means to raise high and elevate. If you are truly ready to get out of your Moab experience and into your Bethlehem season, consider how differently your worship looks knowing that when you humble yourself before the Lord, God will raise you high and elevate you?

God can do all things and do them well, and God's purpose will not be thwarted.[8] Those words, spoken by Job, are a testament to the sovereignty and Lordship of God. Ruth was walking (and humbling herself) in God's plan and purpose for her life. She was willing to do something that was so far from what she knew in her upbringing as a Moabite. She didn't grow up in the church. She didn't go to the temple and worship the sovereign God. She grew up in a community where people did whatever they wanted to do, pleased themselves, and worshiped those little lowercase "g" gods. Even though that was her life growing up, she made a faith decision to not return to that life when given the choice to stay or go with Naomi to Bethlehem. And God honored her choice to make a faith decision.

*God sees you. God loves you.*

What that means for you, starting from right here today, is that if you did not grow up in the church, that won't keep God from having a plan and purpose for your life. God sees you. God loves you. God wants to connect or re-connect with you. If you are willing to trust God and accept God's son, Jesus Christ, as your Lord and Savior, and to make that profession of faith, God will honor your faith decision and will make provisions for you, too. I believe that God will also point you in the right direction of the faith community or church where you can grow in God's word.

Many, many years ago, my mother made a commitment to her then mother-in-law, Myrtha. She promised her that even in the aftermath of a failed marriage to Myrtha's son, that she would still care for her, do what she could to help her son, and always be there for him. And she kept that promise. When circumstances and situations happened that caused Myrtha's son to be placed in a mental health facility, my mother responded and not only advocated for his care, but legally became his guardian. He was medically incapable of making his own decisions. Because Myrtha lived a thousand miles away, she trusted and relied on my mother to stand in the gap and make the tough decisions regarding his well-being. In an interesting turn of events, when Myrtha became ill, and unable to tend to her own health and business matters, my mother responded without hesitation. It was not just the right thing to do – it was the God thing to do.

God has made provision for widows. There is a biblical mandate in which God intends for us to respond to the needs of widows. In fact, Deuteronomy outlines our responsibility to widows, orphans and immigrants. These are our neighbors, our brothers and sisters in Christ, and they need to be cared for, protected and shown the love of Christ just like anyone else. They especially deserve our attention and tending to because of their economic, relational and social vulnerability.

*We're in our new season, yet still living in the past.*

In many ways, as Ruth was making a faith decision to follow Naomi and to accept her mother-in-law's God as her own God, she was also making a commitment to care for a widow. When times got hard, Ruth didn't leave Naomi. Instead, she left her own homeland to follow Naomi, and to walk into a new season of life – one that brought with it uncertainty and all the elements of the unknown, but Ruth pressed through with fearless faith and did it.

She didn't look back at her past; rather, she stayed focused on being in the moment. Many times, we press through our struggles only to constantly remind ourselves of what it was like, where we were, and how bad it was. That takes a lot of energy, focus, worshiping time, and before we know it, we find ourselves mentally back there again. We're in our new season, yet still living in the past from where God brought us. Ruth briefly self-identified as being a foreigner, but only after the men in the field made reference to her Moabite status. Still, she didn't say that she was a Moabite. She simply identified herself as someone not of that town. When you make a decision to follow Christ, there is no reason to identify yourself as the old person that you used to be – you are a new creature in Christ. Christ has forgiven you of those past sins. He is not holding your past against you, and you have to learn how not to hold your past against yourself. There will be people around you who will con- stantly remind you of what you did, when

*Christ has forgiven you of those past sins.*

you did it, and who you did it with. It takes time for people to see the new you. Instead of celebrating the new person that you are, some people will make sly comments like "you've changed," or "you forgot where you came from." It's not that you forgot where you came from; it's that you'd rather forget the situations and circumstances that caused you to be in that Moab experience. As far as them saying that you've changed... you have and you've changed for the better.

## From Barely to Barley

When Ruth and Naomi left Moab, they were in an interesting season of barely making it. Now, here they are in Bethlehem and Ruth is experiencing the favor of God and the fulfillment of God's providential plan. This scene in the barley fields is a historic one because Ruth is receiving all kinds of unexpected privilege, protection and provision. First, she is a woman. Sec- ond, she is a foreigner. And it is unheard of for a non-Israelite to be treated with this kind of favor.

Right now, you might be in a season where you are barely making it. Maybe you are doing all you can to make ends meet. Maybe you are in a dry season at work and you keep watching others get promoted while you get passed over. Maybe your relationship status is barely surviving. There might be contin- uous moments of one hardship after another and it's all you can do to just keep your sanity. Your Moab situation is real. But guess what? Your barley harvest is real, too!

The thing about being in a season of Moab, is that you have to decide that it is only going to be a season. Rather than let the season define you, how do you plan to define who you are *in* it, and more so, who you will be *out* of it? Something has to be different about you when you get to your Bethlehem barley harvest season. Will you be a person who stays stuck in where you were or will you celebrate where you are? Will you wallow in where you have been or will you awaken to the new opportunities that are before you? God wants to do more than just get you out of Moab – God wants to get you out of your Moab mindset. There's not much to reap in your barley harvest if you are still operating like you are barely making it.

*God wants to get you out of your Moab mindset.*

# Be Fearless
## REFLECTION QUESTIONS

**Having authentic worship is one way to move from barely making it in your Moab season to thriving in your barley Bethlehem season. Describe the way you worship God:**

_____

_____

_____

_____

_____

**What is standing in the way of having authentic worship where you bow down before the Lord? Are you more concerned about being embarrassed in front of people or more concerned about being exalted (lifted up) by God?**

_____

_____

_____

_____

_____

_____

_____

# CHAPTER FIVE

# She Walked with Holy Boldness

*"May you be blessed by the Lord, my daughter; this last instance of your loyalty is better than the first; you have not gone after young men, whether poor or rich. And now, my daughter do not be afraid, I will do for you all that you ask, for all the assembly of my people know that you are a worthy woman."*
*— Ruth 3:10-11 —*

One of the things that cannot be denied about this entire narrative of Ruth, is this: the characters in this story make it a point to proclaim God's blessings over one another. As part of a faith community, Naomi, Ruth and now Boaz, speak life and love. It is a testament to not only sharing the Good News of who God is, but it is an intentional step in being a witness to the faith. Each was unafraid to declare God's goodness and was unselfish in doing so. This is important because it shows that when you speak life over someone else, you are not diminishing what God is doing in your own life. When you are willing to offer a kind word of blessings to someone else, it does not take anything away from you. Too often, some people are quick to speak defeat, destruction and doubt over someone's life, and are less likely to speak words of encouragement. Perhaps you have been that person who has heard words like "you're not good enough," "you'll never amount to anything," or "you're just like your no good father or mother." Those words are hurtful, damaging and do nothing to offer the hope and healing that is available to you within the covenant relationship with God. Perhaps, just perhaps, you have uttered those words to someone out of your own disappointment, hurt and frustrations. I want to offer you a new outlook and new perspective – one of walking in holy boldness and speaking words of empowerment over others.

Now that Ruth knows exactly who Boaz is, Naomi makes a bold and somewhat controversial move in what she tells her daughter-in-law to do. There is no way to sugarcoat what seemingly happens in chapter three and there is no way to confirm exactly what happens. The text offers what appears to be innuendos and suggestive remarks. Biblical scholars offer their thoughts of the interplay in this chapter, and they give close examination to the words in their original Hebrew meaning to discern the scene of events, the intentions of the events and the actuality of the events. In other words, the text does not give "beyond a shadow of a doubt" wording that clears up any hypotheticals of what happens between Ruth and Boaz. Let's just say that what appears to happen on the threshing floor, stays on the threshing floor.

I also want to offer as a disclaimer that this narrative is part of God's word. It is part of the history of our humanity as a faith community, as believers, as those who struggle in our faith, and it is an important piece that should not be overlooked, over-analyzed or overshadowed by assumptions.

Naomi is still very determined to help Ruth secure a promising future. In her relentless efforts to "seek some security" for Ruth, this mother-in-law who knows what it is like to be alone and unsure of her future in a male-dominated society, tells Ruth to take the initiative in the next steps of establishing her future. It is also likely why Naomi told her to stay close to the other young women in the field so that she would not be harassed by the men in the field. There is strength in numbers and something powerful happens when women stick together and form a true sense of community and sisterhood.

*Something powerful happens when women stick together.*

## Creating A Movement with Your Faith

In 1938, the community in Saratoga, New York, came to know a widow who pressed through her own calamity with grit and determination to not only make a name for herself, but also a living for herself in the aftermath of her husband's death. Hattie Austin Moseley opened a food stand bearing her name, a chicken shack that offered hungry customers some of the best southern fried chicken, biscuits and other delicious menu items. She learned how to navigate life as a widow, as an entrepreneur and as one who was solely responsible for her livelihood and well-being. Here she was, in the midst of the Great Depression, when the economy was at an all-time low, when businessmen were hitting rock bottom and many were taking their own lives, Hattie showed grit and determination. She wasn't afraid to do the work that it took to survive, and within a year, she turned that food stand into a full-fledge restaurant. It became the "go to" eatery where baseball legend Jackie Robinson frequented, as did musician Cab Calloway. She pushed her way through a season of hardships and ran that restaurant until she was in her nineties. Along the way, she mentored other young women and shared her experiences and gave sage advice on how to press through life's struggles.

Naomi was doing the same thing for Ruth. When she instructed Ruth to "wash and anoint yourself, and put on your best clothes," she was placing her daughter-in-law in a position to secure her future. In the biblical custom of the Israelite community, Boaz was considered the nearest kinsman of

Elimelech. The Hebrew word is *"go'el,"* which means "one with the right to redeem." The kinsman, or *go'el*, had the responsibility of protecting the rights of a family whose "head of household" or husband was absent. In other words, Naomi was not sending Ruth to some random person for a "hook up"; she was sending her to meet with the man who had a biblical and legal responsibility to ensure that Ruth's future was secure. Ruth was in some sense being positioned as the initiator in this encounter with Boaz. It is questionable as to whether Naomi was sending her daughter-in-law into a dangerous situation or a precarious predicament. To ensure that nothing happened against Ruth's will, she was instructed how to protect herself while at the same time protect her future.

It is easy to jump ahead and assume what is happening here, but it is important to read the text for what is there, rather than what is *not* there. This is a very intimate and personal encounter, yes, but intimate does not mean that it was sexual. Intimate means that it was close and private. Naomi's clear directives to Ruth resulted in the young woman initiating a marriage proposal to Boaz, not a prenuptial rendezvous! Verses 8 and 9 capture the excitement of what happened. There was no enticement. "At midnight, the man was startled, and turned over, and there, lying at his feet, was a woman! He said, "Who are you?" And she answered, "I am Ruth, your servant; spread your cloak over your servant, for you are next-of-kin." Was this an invitation for sexual intimacy? Some scholars suggest so because "feet" is often used as a euphemism for male body parts. Again, though, the text does not say outright that there was any sexual intimacy that happened on the threshing floor. Remember, not all of life's experiences are recorded scene by scene.

That took guts. That took grit. That took fearless faith. Ruth could not know what would happen. There she was – at midnight on the threshing floor of all places, negotiating her future. She didn't pause to worry about the what ifs and the

Plan B in case things backfired. She went in hopeful and unhindered. When you walk in holy boldness it will not backfire on you. Walk in the steps that God has ordered and ordained for you. Ruth knew enough to know that compared to what her life had been like just a few short weeks earlier, her faith was bigger than her fear. She knew that God had shown favor on her in the fields and there was no reason to believe that God would not show that same favor in this gutsy move on her part – obedience to what Naomi was telling her to do. Boaz proved to be a man of honor in that he did not take advantage of Ruth. Boaz proved that he was kind in public and in private. The same person that he was in the field is the same person that he was at midnight.

*When you walk in holy boldness it will not backfire on you.*

Once more, Boaz spoke a blessing over Ruth. At midnight. He responded with words of humility, honor and hope. Verse 11 records him as saying: "And now, my daughter, do not be afraid, I will do for you all that you ask, for all the assembly of my people know that you are a worthy woman." Let me pause here and say that I don't know what your season is right now nor do I know how God will show up in your midnight hour. But I do believe that God will show up. God has this unexplainable and amazing way of showing up in the unexpected situations of our lives with a response that is "exceeding abundantly above all that we ask or think, according to the power that is at work in us." That's how it is written in the old King James version of Ephesians 3:20 and I like that wording because it proclaims, from the experience of Apostle Paul, that God is exceeding abundantly. That's what God did for Ruth in this moment. When you look at the way that Boaz responded to her, spoke a blessing over her and promoted her worth as a woman – in a culture and society where a woman's worth had little value – and where as a widow her value had previously been tied to her husband, here he was proclaiming to Ruth in

*God will show up in your midnight hour.*

the midnight hour that all the assembly of his people knew about her worth. That is exceeding abundantly!

The impact and impression that an assembly of people has on you are monumental. It reminds me of the impact that the assembly of women had in the late 1800s when they demonstrated grit, determination and a fierce and fearless drive to make a difference. It was one of the most historic movements and game-changing walks of faith that shaped modern-day history. The Women's Rights Movement where suffragettes marched relentlessly in pursuit of pressing for the right of women to vote in political elections in the United States. Somewhere in Seneca Falls, New York on a hot summer day in 1848, women gathered to break barriers and to change the face of the political landscape. It's hard to imagine now, but at that time, women didn't have the "right" to vote. It was denied to them simply out of gender bias. They were not allowed to have a voice in who would serve them and speak for them in any of the political elections in this country. No vote for president of the United States. No vote for a US Congress member. Not even a vote for mayor of their home city.[9]

Elizabeth Stady Canton and Lucretia Mott were fearless in their approach. History shows that Stanton authored a document titled, "*Declaration of Sentiments, Grievances, and Resolutions*" that somewhat echoed the words of the preamble to the Declaration of Independence. One specific item that was outlined in this declaration was "achieving the sacred right of franchise," or voting. Three years later, in 1851, the abolitionist, author and spokesperson Sojourner Truth, added her fearlessness to the struggle. Each of these women pressed through the struggles of a male-dominated society. They pressed through the hardships. They pressed through the barriers, broke them down, and ultimately their grit, determination and wit, along with the hundreds of women who joined them and fought with their voices, strategy, and ability, made it possible for women to be able to vote in elections today.

These women initiated a movement of change in a system that didn't value their voices. They encountered naysayers and hundreds of people who made it their business to stand in the way of these fearless women. They encountered name-calling and were often ostracized, but they *These women, in the spirit of Ruth, grew through their trials.* were persistent in pressing through their struggles. These women, in the spirit of Ruth, grew through their trials. They strengthened their faith. They realized their power, and they harnessed their inner energy, their collective energy to spring forth with a mighty resilience that could not be reckoned with.

Talk about stepping into your future and stepping over the noise of naysayers!

If you remember early on in Ruth's story, the whole town was stirred when they saw Naomi and her daughter-in-law coming to Bethlehem from Moab. In fact, Ruth was almost a "background image," because the focus of the women's remarks was on Naomi. According to the text, the women didn't utter a word about this young woman, even *You are very much visible to the Lord.* though she was very much present and an integral part in Naomi's return to her homeland of Bethlehem. And it happens that way sometimes. While other people might overlook you, God never does. You are very much visible to the Lord.

In what follows, Ruth was referred to as the Moabite over and over. Any time someone spoke of her, it was with the class and categorization of foreigner and Moabite. Yet in the short amount of time that Ruth had been in Bethlehem during the harvest season, the townspeople had an opportunity to observe her ethics, her character and the way in which she carried herself. She was able to quell the whispers of the naysayers. She shut down the noise and distraction that any potential doubters tried to send her way. She put in the work and she was successful. Who she was now spoke volumes over who she was then. Some people will do their best to try to tie you to your past, and create echoes of who you *used to be*, but God will provide opportunities for you to shine and be seen for the person that you are today. Your struggles and hardships will pay off.

*Your struggles and hardships will pay off.*

I am not promoting or endorsing that you show up somewhere at the midnight hour in a bold move. Your midnight hour might be in a 9 am staff meeting or a 4 pm networking event. When you have spent some time worshiping and honoring God, you will know when it is the right time to make your holy bold move. And God will order your steps and move right along with you.

*Ruth was willing to break the barriers and press forth with fearless faith.*

Ruth did something that perhaps no other woman in recorded biblical history had done. She made her intentions known by requesting that Boaz spread his cloak over her. The cloak was symbolic of protection and covering – the kind of covering that a husband has over his wife. Whether or not Boaz was planning to ask for her hand in marriage, Ruth initiated the suggestion that they marry. Ruth was willing to break the barriers and press forth with fearless faith. She didn't set out to be a trailblazer. She wasn't intentionally being a game-changer, but in the midst of her grit and determination, that's exactly what she did.

*Sometimes we are scarred by our past and it causes us to be scared of our future.*

Right now, wherever you are, you are standing in the shadow of that fearless faith. Let it be your covering that pushes you to not remain in the Moab situation that you are in, but to get to your Bethlehem promise. Sometimes we are scarred by our past and it causes us to be scared of our future. This is your shining moment to be a game-changer. Trust God to change your situation. Trust your faith to change your perspective. Don't get any more settled in your frustrations, fears and disappointments. They've held you long enough. They only have as much power as you give them. Instead of approaching your circumstances with a setback mentality, approach them with a game-changer attitude.

Ruth walked onto that threshing floor with holy boldness. She didn't spend time second-guessing what her mother-in-law instructed her to do. She didn't take time to be afraid or to talk herself out of it. She was purposeful and intentional in her walk. She accomplished with Boaz what she went there to do. You'll notice that Boaz tells her to remain until morning and that it must not be known that a woman had been to the threshing floor. This is because the threshing floor was considered an unsafe environment for women. Drunken men, men looking to steal grain, and men who were looking for a night of "quick fast and in a hurry" interaction with women, often frequented the threshing floor at night because in the still of the night, anything could happen, and the foreign women and widows who might be there could easily be taken advantage of and mishandled against their will.

*God is moving swiftly to secure our future.*

Once more, Boaz was protecting Ruth. He had already stated that she was worthy and he lauded her for the admirable qualities of sticking with Naomi through tough times. It makes sense, then, that Boaz would want to ensure that Ruth remained safe. After all, he was her mother-in-law's next of kin, and now he was potentially Ruth's future husband.

## Walking into Your Future...Now

We never know how God is setting up our future, yet what we do know is that God is already actively involved in orchestrating the details of our future. Often while we are feeling stuck and strapped in the present, unable to let go of some of the painful things of the past, God is moving swiftly to secure our future.

And we can walk into that future if we are willing to walk with holy boldness and trust the God who is there waiting for us.

When my mother was seven years-old, she was affected by a condition that caused her leg to weaken and lose most of its ability to walk. She was suddenly limited by her impairment. Growing up in the 1940's, my mother also faced other limitations. Though her family had access to some privileges, they did not have full access as other families did. She often said that because she was the daughter of a white father and black mother, she had some advantages that black children did not have. And because she was fair-skinned, she was able to go in places with my grandfather that she would not otherwise have been able to go into. Especially in the south. So when her everyday ability to walk became more and more challenging and pronounced, my grandfather took her from Texas to Oklahoma to see a doctor whose specialty was working with children and adults who had what was termed a "crippled leg."

It was confirmed that my mother had polio. At seven.

In order to strengthen her leg and ensure that she'd be able to walk as normally as a seven-year-old should, my mother had to wear an iron brace on her leg. It slowed her down. It gave cause for other kids to tease her and give her the unwanted nickname of "Iron Leg." It was uncomfortable and it temporarily interrupted her childhood. For three years, she wrangled with that brace. For three years, she had to go back and forth to the doctor and lay in an iron tube that came all the way up to her waist. It was so that her bone could be strengthened. She said the noise that the machine made sounded a lot like water swishing and swashing around in a tub.

For three years, my mother had to drag her leg. She couldn't go very far, even with that iron brace on it, but she was determined to walk normally again. She had grit. Even as a little kid. She had fierce determination and a fearless kind of strength. And then one day, in the spring of 1950, when she was ten, my mother removed that brace.

And she walked.

She walked with holy boldness. She walked with fearless faith. She pressed through her struggles. Pressed through the teasing. Pressed through the name-calling.

*She walked with holy boldness.*

With holy boldness, my mother walked with a previously weakened leg that was now stronger than ever. With holy boldness, she was able to play again with her siblings and the other kids at school. With holy boldness, she was able to run.

My mother was spurred on by grit, determination and a fearless kind of faith. She went on to become a game-changer on the basketball court in high school, leading her team to many victories as the center guard. She didn't let the pain of her past keep her from the promising future that God had for her. And that experience helped her walk with holy boldness through many other tough times in her life that sought to cripple her – like discrimination, biases and the ugliness of racism.

In his letter to the Ephesians, Apostle Paul reminds us that through Christ Jesus, "we have access to God in boldness and confidence through faith in him" (Ephesians 3:12). Think about what this means for your Moab situation. Because of your covenant relationship with Jesus – because you believe that Christ died for your sins – because you believe that God wants the best for you – you have access to the God who is the Creator of the universe. And this access is in boldness. That means that you can tell your Moab situation about the God who has power over your situation. Add to that confidence, through faith, and you have enough grit to get to your Bethlehem promise!

# Be Fearless

## REFLECTION QUESTIONS

**Describe the tough situation that are you walking through?**

_____

_____

_____

_____

_____

**In what ways do you feel limited in your situation? Write a one-sentence prayer of what you need from God in order to walk boldly through and out of your Moab situation. Be specific and tell the Lord exactly what you need.**

_____

_____

_____

_____

_____

# CHAPTER SIX

# She Said Yes and Experienced God's Best

*"He said, "Who are you?" And she answered,*
*"I am Ruth, your servant."*
*— Ruth 3:9 —*

I believe that sometimes the biggest hurdle we must overcome is our fear of saying yes. We've been accustomed to hearing no for so long that it scares us to hear yes. Yes to happiness. Yes to success. Yes to goodness. Yes.

If you've heard God's calling on your life, then you probably know what it's like to be afraid to say yes. Whether God is calling you to be a pediatric nurse where your giftedness will help to heal babies and children, or God is calling you to be a certified public accountant where you will help people and companies to be fiscally healthy, there is a likelihood that saying yes to all that this entails comes with a resounding fear of saying yes.

And if you've ever wanted to say yes, but someone crushed it with a no, that makes it even more difficult to muster up the courage again to move forward in your calling.

In the spring of 2000, I was actively engaged in my church. I was involved in ministry, growing in my worship and prayer life, and finally paying attention to the nudging and prompting from God that it was time to take seriously the calling that God had on my life for ordained ministry. I remember scheduling a meeting with my senior pastor. I went into that meeting, filled with hope, hesitation and yet a strong willingness to finally say out loud beyond the perimeter of my living room, that God had called me to preach and I was ready to move forward.

And that's when my yes was crushed with a resounding no from my pastor, the person who was the shepherd and spiritual leader of the church where I had been a member for a few years. I still remember his response, because it has framed my ministry, and has caused me to walk with holy boldness in the midst of the naysayers: "God didn't call you into ministry. You heard God wrong. God doesn't call women. I suggest you go back and pray and ask what did God *really* say to you."

*Really*? Ouch!

I left that meeting crushed. I left that meeting second-guessing God. I left that meeting so deflated and puzzled. To be told that I heard God wrong was a response that I had never imagined in a thousand years.

I am confident, though, that God continued to say yes. God said yes when I applied to seminary many years later, and stepped into my calling. God said yes when I left a lucrative career as a regional vice president of communications and marketing for a well-known national non-profit that is dedicated to educating the community on their risks for heart disease and stroke. God said yes when I graduated magna cum laude from Southern Methodist University with my Master's Degree in Theological Studies and a concentration in church history. God said yes when I began serving full-time as a pastor in a denomination that didn't bat an eye or tell you how wrong you were for being a woman with a calling for pastoral leadership and a vision to help lead God's people from brokenness to wholeness.

I walked in holy boldness and God said yes every step of the way. Sure, those "yeses" came with some struggles, hurdles and doors to kick in and barriers to break down, but because God was saying yes, I knew that it didn't matter if I heard a loud "no" along the way. I was confident that God would make a way for me to still ful-fill my calling, share the Good News and usher people from those broken places to the healing and wholeness that God had waiting for them.

*There is a "yes" in your life that God has already stamped with God's approval.*

And I am confident that there is a "yes" in your life that God has already stamped with God's approval, that the Lord is waiting for you to respond to and walk in.

I believe that every woman has the capacity to embody the spirit of Ruth's determination, grit and fearlessness. Her story is more than just a beautifully told illustration of finding her Boaz. It is a testimony of inspiration within the despera-tion of experiences that we all encounter. And more so, this story is permanently inked in the Bible as our push to hope, our push to dream, our push to keep pressing forward and to strive toward the "yes" that God has designed us for. It's about the promise that awaits us when we make a faith decision to follow God. It's about aligning ourselves in humility with God's plan and purpose for our lives, and what

*The only way for you to experience God's best is to say yes.*

it means to truly worship God in the midst of our difficult sit-uations. Yes, it is so much more than just a woman finding the man of her dreams; it is about finding hope and wholeness after we've been scarred by some painful and heart-breaking experiences in life.

The only way for you to experience God's best is to say yes. And to press forward through the struggles with fearless faith.

You might not know it, but Ruth pressed through a major struggle that evening at the threshing floor. You recall from ear-lier, that the threshing floor was considered unsafe – especially at night when those who were in charge were asleep. Boaz admonished Ruth to leave from there early in the morning so that no one would know that a woman had been there. I think this reasoning is two-fold: first, so that her reputation would not be unfairly tainted, since it could easily be broadcasted that some promiscuous activity had taken place between Ruth and Boaz; and second, so that it would not be assumed that the threshing floor became a place where women gleaners would rest from their labors at night and open themselves to unwanted attention.

*We are walking boldly, in the shadow of prayer.*

If you read the text slowly, even aloud, you will notice this in 3:14, "...but {she} got up before one person could recognize another; for he {Boaz} said, 'it must not be known that the woman came to the threshing floor.'"

Other people were there!

*You've been frozen in fear and afraid to stand on faith.*

Ruth managed to get to Boaz, boldly propose to him, and do so in a private moment while other people were there. God protected the private moment. God knew the intentions and worthiness of Ruth's heart. God also knew the intentions and honor of Boaz's heart. This is to say that, sometimes we can find ourselves in the midst of what can be deemed an unsafe place, yet still experience the safety of God's provision. We can find ourselves in what others would view as a comprising situation, but press through it because we know that God knows we are not compromising anything. We are not compromising our value, our worth, or our reputation. We are walking boldly, in the shadow of prayer, and doing what God has called us to do.

*You have the strength and the capacity to walk in holy boldness!*

We are being like Ruth – pressing through life's struggles with fearless faith.

I've witnessed times when people are pressing through their struggles, and standing on faith, rather than standing frozen in fear. There might be times when you've been frozen in fear and afraid to stand on faith. Hear these words: You have the strength and the capacity to walk in holy boldness! Don't be surprised, though, that others might not recognize your newly found strength. They will ask: Who are you! It's more so out of surprise and awe and less about your identity. In this text, in verse nine, Boaz asks a question: Who are you? He asks this of the Moabite woman. The foreigner. The widow. And then Ruth answers: I am Ruth, your servant.

This same conversation of few words can easily be applied to our talks with God. What if God were to ask today, "Who are you?" What would your response be? It's not that God is asking *who* you are in terms of your name or identity because God obviously knows that – God created you, and formed you in your mother's womb – so God already knows who you are. Rather, God is asking are you a prayer warrior? Are you a worshiper? Are you a person who worries? Are you more doubt-filled than faith-filled? God wants you to be able to see yourself through God's eyes. To see the dynamic and wonderfully made person that God designed you to be. Under all the muck and mire of disappointment, frustration, fear and "I'm so fed up and over this," that dynamic person is still there. Under the heap of "no" that you've heard for so long, that wonderfully made person is still there. Are you ready to tell God, "I am your servant?"

When confronted by Boaz, Ruth didn't cower in fear. She didn't lose her composure. She didn't lose sight of her purpose for being there. She answered Boaz with boldness. She answered the prominent leader with fierceness. She answered with a resounding sense of confidence in who she was and who she wanted to become. She was Ruth. The foreigner. The Moabite. The daughter-in-law of Naomi. But who she wanted to become was Boaz's wife. She was ready to leave her status of widow and upgrade it to wife.

Boaz accepted Ruth for who she was and embraced who she wanted to become, but he did not rush ahead and begin to set things in motion. Instead he made Ruth aware of another relative who might have "first dibs" on her hand in marriage. Yes, Boaz was a kinsman of Elimelech, Ruth's now deceased father-in-law, but there was also another man who was a relative – one who was more closely related than Boaz. And in this continuous display of humility and honor, this is yet one more admirable act from Boaz. He chose to wait, notify the other relative, and then to – yes, you guessed it, wait for the response.

In the meantime, he gave Ruth six measures of barley. He placed it in her cloak, and then put it on her back. Ruth had a cloak. Boaz had a cloak. You may recall from reading earlier in this chapter that Ruth asked Boaz to spread his cloak over her. Biblically, the garment was used in a declaration of one's intentions for a lifelong relationship. Think of it in modern-day terms as an engagement ring – it is a public and private way of saying that you and this person are together now with plans to finalize the togetherness from this day forward.

So, in an interesting twist, Boaz takes the cloak that Ruth is wearing, fills it with barley and does so in the same way that a husband or provider would do. In essence, Boaz was playing an active role as provider even though he knew that another relative – one who Ruth did not know and had never even heard of – had the opportunity to "be with Ruth from this day forward." He was insistent though that Ruth not return home empty-handed.

*I love how God will bring things full circle.*

I love how God will bring things full circle. Back in chapter one, Naomi expressed how she went away full (leaving Bethlehem and moving to Moab) and the Lord brought her back empty. And now, here she is, with her fearless daughter-in-law, with six measures of barley! Regardless to how things might turn out while Boaz waits to make contact with the nearest kinsman, Naomi will have plenty to eat. There's nothing worse than waiting to hear news on an empty stomach. God, who is always working behind the scenes, in front of the scenes and right there *on the scene*, made sure that Ruth and Naomi had food to eat. From the moment that Naomi and Ruth walked into the town of Bethlehem, God made sure they were fed. Nowhere in the text does it say anything about them missing a meal, going hungry or being famished. Psalm 37:25 assures us that when we are in covenant relationship with the Lord, God always takes care of our nourishment needs. "I have been young and now I am old, yet I have not seen the righteous forsaken or their children begging for bread."

Ruth and Naomi's time of waiting was well spent – they had food to eat while Boaz made contact with the nearest kinsman. In fact, Naomi tells Ruth to wait until she learns how the matter will turn out. The text doesn't specifically say what Ruth should *not* do while waiting. We can surmise that Ruth was so hopeful and excited in telling her mother-in-law about what happened at the threshing floor. It is also likely that in all the excitement, Ruth started projecting forward about her plans with Boaz. About what her life would be like as his wife. About how Naomi's future would be secured as well. This is where the phrase, "don't count your chickens until your eggs hatch" comes to mind. It's so easy for us to get excited and begin to jump ahead in our preparations, that we don't slow down and do the "prayer"-parations that are necessary to make sure that we are still following God's plan and not detouring to our own plans. It is not wrong to get excited. It is not wrong to be bursting at the seams about the possibility of a new outcome. Not at all. It's perfectly fine to be happy and joyous. It is important, though, to make sure that the happiness doesn't overshadow what God wants us to do while we are waiting.

## A Pioneering Kind of Faith

Ruth was living in a time when agriculture was the occupation of the day. While women during biblical times were largely not recorded as working in the fields, or shepherding, in a sense

Ruth was a pioneer for her fearless efforts. And she led the way for other fearless pioneers in the field of agriculture.

Dolores Clara Fernandez Huerta was the daughter of a farm worker and miner in New Mexico in the 1930s who understood the labor that went into agricultural work. She also understood and witnessed the economic disparity of Mexican, Filipino, Japanese, Chinese and African American families who lived in the same agricultural community where she and her family lived. Huerta also witnessed many of the children of these farm workers, going to school with growling stomachs, and walking barefoot on the sidewalks of Stockton, California, because shoes were a luxury that their families could not afford. Huerta looked beyond what was in front of her and imagined the possibilities that were beyond her. Her vision, grit and determination, coupled with her sheer sense of foresight and compassion, led her to found the Agricultural Workers Association. [10] To her, the families who labored in the fields were more than just poor, low-income wage earners; they were people who deserved to experience the greatness that God had in store for them. It was during this time, in the 1950s, that she met and befriended César Chávez; in 1962, they launched the National Farm Workers Association. Because Huerta was willing to step in the places that women had not occupied before, and endure the challenges and hardships that came with it, she was able to lobby for farm workers. She is credited with having an integral part in the Agricultural Labor Relations Act of 1975, which was the first law dedicated to making sure that farm workers in California were afforded the right and privilege to come together and organize for more wages and better working conditions. Like, Ruth, Huerta knew the struggles of agricultural life and the weight it had on the people who worked tirelessly in the fields, but she pressed through the hardships and made a difference for countless families and she made a meaningful impact on the lives of people everywhere – all because she was willing to look past just what was possible and see what was there in the impossible. She knew when to press and she knew when to wait.

One of the things that I have learned and truly appreciate about God is that there will be times when God simply says "Wait."

*She knew when to press and she knew when to wait.*

Wait, my daughter, or wait, my son. God will give this directive because God doesn't want us to rush ahead of God's plans. I learned a long time ago that we operate in *chronos* time, meaning the chronological and sequential order of time – Tuesday follows Monday, Wednesday follows Tuesday and so forth. We know that this "timing" will not change. God operates in *kyros* time – meaning that God is already ahead in the future, five years down the road, looking at what will happen then, and working things out now, so that when the "then" comes, our waiting will have been worth it. God's *kyros* time is indeterminate. Our waiting will have been in direct alignment with what God has planned. Our waiting will have been a time of growing and strengthening our faith.

# Be Fearless
## REFLECTION QUESTIONS

What is your faith status right now? Is it doubtful, hopeful, fearful? Write what you are feeling and then share a two or three-sentence prayer to God asking God to show you, through God's eyes, that you are dynamic and wonderfully made.

_____

_____

_____

_____

_____

What "status" are you willing and ready to give up in order to say yes and experience God's best?

_____

_____

_____

List at least three things that you will do while you are waiting to experience God's best, now that you have said "yes."

_____

_____

_____

_____

# CHAPTER SEVEN

# She is Fearless!

*"Then all the people who were at the gate,*
*along with the elders, said, we are witnesses."*
— *Ruth 4:11* —

God always lines up the right people, in the right place and at the right time. This marketplace scene in chapter four is a para-court room of sorts where legal and binding agreements take place. Whenever God puts God's plan in motion, you can rest assured that things will go according to the Lord's plan. The very fact that God *is doing* something is a binding, unbreakable agreement in itself. And it's even more fascinating when people are present to witness the greatness that God is doing.

*Witness the greatness that God is doing.*

Naomi's closing words in chapter three indicated that Boaz would not rest until this matter had been taken care of – this matter of which kinsman would have the rightful and lawful legal claim to Ruth. This is a serious matter. To read and be a witness to what is happening in this scene further illustrates the rewards that come with pressing through life's struggles with fearless faith.

One such woman, who I surmise had the grit, determination and willingness to press through like Ruth, is Constance Baker Motley. Before she made history as the first African American woman to hold a federal judgeship, when President Lyndon Baines Johnson appointed her to the United States District Court in 1966, she had to press through some challenging situations to make her mark.

When she was just fifteen, she made up in her mind to pursue studies in law and become a lawyer, after reading that Abraham Lincoln had pronounced the legal field as one of the most challenging professions. That dream was temporarily halted following her graduation from high school because her family's financial situation did not allow her to attend college right away. Her parents, who had emigrated from the West Indies, made their home in Connecticut and began having children. With nine children to raise, they demonstrated that hard work and determination pays off. Motley's mother, Rachel Baker, founded the New Haven, Connecticut branch of the National Association for the Advancement of Colored People. Her father, Willoughby Alva Baker, was a chef at Yale University.

Undeterred by her family's financial hardship, Motley worked as a maid, then with the National Youth Administration. She used every opportunity to get one step closer to her dream. In fact, it was during an event where she gave such a compelling speech, that a wealthy white businessman heard her and offered to pay her college tuition. She enrolled at Fisk University and completed her studies at New York University, earning a degree in economics. This was in the early 1940s when women of color did not necessarily have many advantages to succeed. In 1944, her family, friends and the university community were witnesses as she became the first African American woman accepted to the Columbia School of Law. They also witnessed more of God's greatness as Motley worked with civil rights lawyer Thurgood Marshall. In 1954, America witnessed her brilliance when she became the first

African American female attorney to argue a case before the US Supreme Court. She was part of the team of lawyers in the landmark *Brown v. Board of Education of Topeka* case, that forever changed public school education, making it unlawful to segregate children in public schools based on race, because to do so violated the Equal Protection Clause of the Fourteenth Amendment of the Constitution.

*She fought for justice.*

Motley had grit. Her sheer determination significantly impacted the lives of so many people. She fought for justice. She fought for Freedom Riders in the 1960s. She fought for other people of color who simply wanted the same opportunities afforded to their white counterparts. And American history bears witness to her hardships, to her struggles and to her fierceness of pressing through with fearless faith. Over eight decades, from 1921 to 2005, God had a powerful plan and purpose for Motley's life that benefitted not just her, but generations of people. Even in the moments when the possible looked impossible and not at all probable, Motley's dream of having a career in law was not interrupted. She is quoted as saying, "I rejected the notion that my race or sex would bar my success in life."[11]

*There are some people who need to be witnesses to your grit.*

In chapter one, things looked grim for Ruth. I'm sure as a young woman that she had dreams, hopes and desires. When her husband died, it is easy to assume that her dreams and hopes died, too. But that might not necessarily be true. I believe that whatever the dreams are that God has planted and placed inside of you, they are still there. So, what about you and your dreams? Maybe your situation has drastically changed and you feel so far removed from your dreams. Hardships have knocked at your door one too many times. Don't give up. There are some people who need to be witnesses to your grit, to your determination and to your fearless faith.

We all have life challenges that parallel the angst and anxiety that are building up in this scene in chapter four. Ruth's future hinges on what happens in this interplay with the nearest kinsman. Have you ever been so anxious about something that you projected ahead in a doubtful way of what *might* happen? Then you started operating out of what *might* happen? Then you made plans based on what *might* happen? Then you started having conversations with your trusted friends and family members about all the things that *might* happen, to the point that you overlooked what was actually happening? It seems like far too often we live in the "might happen" of doubts rather than the assurance of our faith.

*Too often we live in the "might happen" of doubts rather than the assurance of our faith.*

From what we can tell in the text, this was not the case for Ruth. She didn't project ahead at any time with any sense of doubt. From the moment that we were introduced to her, to her journey from the depressing situation in Moab to the hopeful promise in Bethlehem, not once did we see any semblance of doubt on her part. Ruth was brand new in the faith, of believing in the sovereign God, and she led her life in an encouraging faith-filled way for which we can take notice and learn. With every faith step that she took, Ruth erased bits of her painful past. When she arrived in Bethlehem and made her way to the fields to glean, Ruth wore the label of foreigner, Moabite and widow. Within days, though, her strength, fortitude and character made an impression on Boaz and others in the city. It was so impressive that she became known as a woman of worth. The dismissive labels of foreigner and Moabite were gone. She was now walking in her purpose and in this new life that God had waiting for her. She only needed to press through her struggles with fearless faith to get there. When we get to that place of trusting God completely with the life that God has

*She was now walking in her purpose.*

given us, that is, the one that the Lord breathed the first breath of air into, then we can begin to see the great things revealed that God has for us.

God had greatness in store for Ruth. Her future is further revealed by what happens at the city gate. Boaz arrives at this

*Ruth didn't operate in what was just possible.*

commercial center where business and legal transactions take place, and the next-of-kin also arrives. Boaz does not waste any time inviting the unnamed kinsman to have a seat so that he can be made aware of what is at stake. It is in this conversation that we learn something else: Naomi is selling a parcel of land that belonged to Elimelech. This is yet another surprising act of power and position by a woman during a time when women didn't have the means nor the societal approval to authorize business transactions. Yet it is a testimony to imagining the possibilities and believing in God's capabilities. God is able! It reminds me of something that author and former poet laureate Rita Dove is credited with saying: "You have to imagine it possible before you can see something. You can have the evidence right in front of you, but if you can't imagine something that has never existed before, it's impossible."[12]

Ruth didn't operate in what was just possible. She ventured into the impossible and she revealed that God meets us there, too! When it seemed impossible that she could have a fulfilling life following the death of her husband, Ruth pressed forward and made a big decision to follow Naomi. When it seemed impossible that she could put food on the table, Ruth worked in those barley fields and proved herself to be a "breadwinner," with the heaps of barley that she brought home for herself and her mother-in-law. When it seemed impossible that she would be able to move beyond the label of being a Moabite, a foreigner, and a widow, she gained the respect of the Israelites and earned the title as a worthy woman. If you only do what is possible, you will never see the fullness of what is available and waiting for you in the impossible. God is there and ready to meet you in the impossible.

*God is there and ready to meet you in the impossible.*

Boaz has a very matter-of-fact conversation with the kinsman in verse four. He gives the relative an opportunity to take the land, redeem it, and do so in the presence of "those sitting here, and in the presence of the elders of my {Boaz's} people." If the redeeming is to take place, it must be handled right then and there. There are some decisions that we have to make immediately. God knows that, given the chance, we will squander away the promptness of time and think through all the reasons that we should or should not do something – and in the midst of it, we sometimes miss the blessing in it.

The kinsman responds affirmatively and declares that he will redeem the land. It is at this point that Boaz reveals something else: "The day you acquire the field from the hand of Naomi, you are also acquiring Ruth the Moabite, the widow of the dead man, to maintain the dead man's name on his inheritance." Those words seemed to stun the relative because he reneges on the offer and instead says in verse six that, "I cannot redeem it for myself without damaging my own inheritance. Take my right of redemption for yourself, for I cannot redeem it." And with that, the matter was handled. He removed his sandal, as was customary in Israel whenever a business transaction of redeeming and exchange took place, and gave it to Boaz. The story of Ruth is most often associated with the relationship between her and Boaz, where Boaz is referred to as the "kinsman redeemer." While it is true that Boaz owns this title, it cannot be overlooked that the unnamed relative almost became the kinsman redeemer, and for a few moments, he, too, wore that title. The relative was willing to take the blessing of the land but not what he saw as the burden of the bride who would come with it. For whatever reason, he believed that Ruth would compromise his inheritance and that was something that he was not willing to negotiate.

What God has for you, is for you. You may have had some experiences where you felt that someone else "took" your blessing; but that is not true. God doesn't take your blessing and give it to someone else. Nor does God take someone else's blessing and give it to you. When you are willing to trust God, trust God's timing and operate in fearless faith, you will experience your big reveal.

*What God has for you, is for you.*

In 1967, actress Diahann Carroll received a call from her agent that a producer for NBC was working on developing a sitcom about a black woman. The producer had spoken to a lot of actresses about the role and surprisingly he wasn't interested in Carroll because he felt that she was too sophisticated. The poised and professional person of was not part of this producer's plan for the ground-breaking television show, but Carroll was every bit part of God's vision for this barriers-breaking movement that would forever change the face of television. For the first time, network television was portraying a black woman in a starring role – not as a domestic or mammy but as a professional – a Vietnam War widow who worked as a nurse in the aerospace industry and was mom to a budding five-year old son. This television show, *Julia*, defied many ghetto-tized stereotypes of black women in America, although the producer had peppered the script with the N-word, the same word that arouses and ignites a fire storm in our communities today. You see his plan was to show a different side of black America but at the same time show that the consciousness of America had not yet progressed in their attitudes, beliefs and behaviors toward black women. But Diahann Carroll couldn't envision herself playing *that* Julia. And more so she couldn't imagine that this is what God had envisioned. So she felt empowered enough to demand changes to the script. After the pilot aired in 1967, the show received the nod for 13 episodes and began its three-year run in 1968 during a season of situations and circumstances that seemingly tried to crush God's vision for what Miss Carroll would do in this starring role as *Julia*. There were riots in the inner city, the assassination of Dr. Martin Luther King, Jr., followed by the assassination of Senator Robert F. Kennedy that same year, yet God's vision was not shot down. *Julia* went on to become the number one show and received the highest rankings from the Nielsen reports. God's vision was greater than the producer's plans. That vision made room for the future Claire Huxtables of the television industry. Whatever it is that God is showing you and empowering you to do, know that God is equipping you. Your God-given vision comes with God-ordered steps. Diahann Carroll's longevity in television and film was secured in her big reveal as *Julia*.

*What if we begin to look at our lives as part of a generational blessing?*

## Let God Negotiate Your Business

Ruth's future was secured in the exchange of that sandal. Although she was not present to see it, many others were witnesses to God's plan for her. Not only did they witness it, but they also pronounced a generational blessing upon her with these words in verses 11 and 12: "May the Lord make the woman who is coming into your house like Rachel and Leah, who together built the house of Israel. May you produce children in Ephrathah and bestow a name in Bethlehem; and through the children that the Lord will give you by this young woman, may your house be like the house of Perez, whom Tamar bore to Judah."

If we are honest with ourselves, sometimes we look at our situation, our family tree, and easily believe that there is a generational curse on us. What if we begin to look at our lives as part of a generational blessing? What if we knew that our great grandparents pronounced a blessing over our grandparents, parents and us? How would that make you look at your struggles differently? Would you feel the power that is within you, and use it to press through your struggles with fearless faith?

# Be Fearless
## REFLECTION QUESTIONS

What is the one thing that you think is *just* possible, yet you recognize that you need the fearless faith to believe in what lies in the impossible?

_____

_____

_____

Name something that God has done in your life already that demonstrates that God is able to do the impossible?

_____

_____

_____

Ruth was not present when the big reveal happened that led to her blessing. How important is it to you to be present when God sets up your breakthrough, with a crowd of people who will be witnesses, and will tell the story about what God has done for you?

_____

_____

_____

_____

# CHAPTER EIGHT

# The Big Reveal in Finding Your Roots

*"So Boaz took Ruth and she became his wife. When they came together, the Lord made her conceive, and she bore a son."*
— *Ruth 4:13* —

For all that Ruth has endured, pressed through and sacrificed – for all of the hardships and struggles that she encountered, it is all paying off with the blessing that is birthed out of it. Her faith journey was worth it and it is an inspiration for us to keep journeying through whatever we are pressing *through* so that we can get *to* the promise that God has for us.

Earlier I mentioned that what Ruth was doing would bless generations to come, and here it is: The son to whom she gave birth to would grow up to become the father of a man named Jesse. And Jesse would grow up to have several sons, one of whom was hand-picked and anointed by God to become king of Israel – a shepherd boy by the name of David. That's right. Ruth is the great grandmother of King David. We never quite know who is in our ancestral line and what God's plan and purpose for a relative back then, means for us today.

What if I told you that the strength that you need for the hardships and struggles that you are facing today is found in the genealogy of where you came from? When Ruth gave birth to Obed, this son was not just a blessing for her and Boaz, but it was a blessing for Naomi as well. Her family name and lineage would now be able to continue. When it looked like Naomi's livelihood, legacy and any future generation had died in Moab with the deaths of her two sons, God had a plan and purpose far greater than what Naomi could conceive. The Lord caused Ruth to conceive a son so that generations would be blessed - not just the generations of Naomi's family, but the generations that would lead to the birth of Jesus. Peek over in the New Testament and read the first chapter of the Gospel of Matthew. It opens with the genealogy of Jesus and the big reveal is that Boaz, Ruth and Obed are named in the family history. In other words, this story of Ruth's courage, of leaving her spiritually starved life in Moab and moving to the spiritually nourishing community of Bethlehem, set the course for the family tree that led to the birth of our Lord and Savior.

Yes, Ruth's journey was worth it and we are who we are today in Christ because of it!

I recently had an opportunity to trace my family history, on my father's side, with the help of the resource center at the Reginald F. Lewis Museum of African American History and Culture in Baltimore. I happened to be in town to see my best friend. At the museum, I was making my way through the exhibits when one of the employees gave me a flier with the words, "Find Your Roots at the Resource Center," and told me that I could learn how to trace and track my family history. She invited me to the fourth floor to learn more about it. I almost didn't accept her offer because I was planning to make another stop before meeting my friend for dinner that evening. I didn't know at the time that this invitation would lead to a promising revelation. It made me think of how many times we are so busy that we don't recognize the invitation that God is extending to us. And when we miss it, we also miss a critical piece of what is needed to help us along our journey.

Part of my reason for being in Baltimore was to surprise my best friend for her birthday. The other part of being there was to simply get away, regroup, and do some self-care after going through a very traumatic experience in my ministry setting where I was repeatedly the victim of what can best be described as continuous "unwanted touch" by a member of the church. The situation became so bad that I had to involve the police. As a pastor, whose primary role is to walk people through their faith journey, my own faith journey had been significantly impacted by this man who had a history of approaching women and finding ways to make unwanted physical contact. When this person entered my office, and lunged at me one evening as I was preparing for Bible study, all sorts of things ran through my mind: What if this person assaulted me? How could I free myself from my office since this person was blocking the door? And of course, the obvious question of "Why is this happening to me?" I had only been in this ministry setting for a few months. Like some of the other women in history that you've read about in these pages, I, too, was the first African American – the first one to serve as a clergy in that church's 130-year history.

*As a pastor, my own faith journey had been significantly impacted.*

That is a challenge that no one is prepared for and one that no one expects to happen. After enduring and surviving that night's ordeal and surviving the whole four-month experience of repeatedly being the victim of unwanted touch – after saying no, after reporting it time and time again to the senior pastor, and being told to "set boundaries in a way that would not agitate him," I was now wearing another title for the first time in my life – survivor of what the police termed "sexual assault – unwanted touch." And as you can imagine, I was feeling some kind of way.

So, this trip of self-care and spending time with by "bestie" was super important. I had gone through a traumatic and damaging experience and needed to begin the healing process. Part of the healing came in learning about the strength of my great-great-great grandmother. Little did I know that by accepting the invitation to trace my family history, I would find that my great-great-great grandmother endured some hardships of her own. According to the 1880 census, she was 30 years old, with three sons, ranging in ages ten to fourteen, and she owned a farmstead. She was listed as a black woman, the daughter of a mulatto mother and black father. She was also a widow. The more I looked at the census records, the more I could see that she must have had the same kind of grit, determination and fearless faith as Ruth to press through her struggles. *She was a black woman who owned her own farmstead.* Seventeen years following the Emancipation Proclamation, my great-great-great grandmother owned land – as a widow. She didn't have to glean in someone else's fields – she had her own field. I am certain that it took an immeasurable amount of strength to be a widow in 1880 with three young sons. It took strength to carry the role and title of "head of household." Records show that she traveled from Mississippi to Texas. Perhaps, at the time, she and my great-great-great grandfather were in search of a better life. I know from what the records show, all of her sons were born in Texas. I don't know what happened to her husband. The narrative of the census doesn't reveal that, but I do know that he made it to Texas because all of their sons were born in Texas.

I also know from census records that her mother, who was also listed as a widow, lived on the farmstead, too. Somehow, they had ended up in Texas. I have no idea how long it took to get there, when or why the decision was made to "head west" from Mississippi, or what mode of transportation they used

> I had gone through a traumatic and damaging experience and needed to begin the healing process.

for their journey. The big reveal, though, is that both women were finding favor in God's sight. They were in charge of their livelihood, making their own decisions, and raising and protecting the lives of three black boys.

There is an inner strength that emerges in finding your roots. There is an inherent sense of grit, determination and fearless faith that is embedded in your family's DNA. There is something profound and remarkably life-giving knowing that whatever hardship and struggle you find yourself in, that somewhere in your family tree, you had a great relative who endured, who survived their own Moab season and thrived in their Bethlehem harvest. I don't know all the particular details about my ancestors' journey, but what I do know is that we are cut from the same cloth. Ninety years after that census was taken, I made my mark for the first time on a census as the daughter of a family rooted in grit and determination.

*The big reveal, though, is that both women were finding favor in God's sight.*

I am my great-great-great grandmother's descendant. Her strength, grit and determination was passed down to me. And when the traumatic experience in my ministry setting sought to paralyze me, I had to remember that the strength that my own mother had, overcoming polio and the inability to use her leg, was also passed down to me. Grit and strength runs in my family!

*Her strength, grit and determination was passed down to me.*

Ruth's son, Obed, was rooted in a family of struggle, hardship, grit and determination. His birth brought about healing and restoration for Naomi. Interestingly, his name means worshipper. Though the women named him Obed, it is fitting that his name is a testimony of who Ruth became in her faith journey. She became a worshipper of the sovereign God.

# Be Fearless

## REFLECTION QUESTIONS

**Now that you are at the end of this story about Ruth's fearless faith, grit and determination, what do you believe God is showing you as your big reveal?**

_____

_____

_____

_____

_____

**Whose strength can you pull from in your family history to help you through your hardships and struggles? Write something about their journey so that it can inspire you in your journey.**

_____

_____

_____

_____

_____

_____

# Conclusion

We all have hardships, struggles, disappointments, and frustrations, regardless of where we are in our faith journey. We all have that one Moab experience that hit us harder than we expected. It happens to the seasoned saint as well as to the newcomer in Christ.

Your faith journey deserves all the grit, strength and determination that is available to you through your relationship with Christ Jesus. There will be low moments that seek to set you back, but remember to use these moments to make your comeback. Comeback with a stronger prayer life. Comeback as an authentic worshipper. Comeback stronger in studying God's word. Comeback with a fierceness to get to your barley harvest season. The story of Ruth is written in four chapters, but the overall journey is much more than that. I don't know where you are in your chapter, but I do know that God loves you, cares for you, and desires the best for you. Don't be discouraged by your struggles and don't let go of the God who is right there with you. Remember that your hardships can help you to hold on more tightly to God's unchanging hand. It takes work to move from your Moab experience to your Bethlehem promise. As we've explored and uncovered in this story, the first step begins with making the decision that you are tired of being in Moab. The next step is trusting God, being obedient to what God is telling you to do (what lines up with Scripture), and then actually preparing yourself for the journey. You can't get to *there*, if you are set on staying *here*.

Finally, think of how your faith journey will inspire someone else. I am a firm believer that God never wastes an experience. God can take the very thing that the enemy meant for evil, and turn it around and use it for good. God can move you from Moab to "Mo Better."

I never said that being Ruth is easy; but being like her is doable. I will be praying for you as you press through your struggles with fearless faith.

# Notes

---

1. forbes.com/sites/margaretperlis/2013/10/29/5-characteristics-of-grit-what-it-is-why-you-need-it-and-do-you-have-it/#4f100c4e1f76 (accessed October 2016)

2. The story of Esther Elizabeth McCready resources from the Reginald F. Lewis Museum of African American History and Culture in Baltimore, Maryland and http://msa.maryland.gov/msa/educ/exhibits/womenshall/html/mccready.html; accessed December 12, 2016

3. thekingcenter.org/blog/mlk-quote-week-faith-taking-first-step (accessed October 26, 2016)

4. Psalm 141:9 New International Version

5. Psalm 139: 14

6. Deuteronomy 24: 20-21 gives some very specifics about the Christian's response to care for the widows, orphans, homeless (sojourners) and foreigners; God mandates that Christians allow them to glean in the fields and receive the food that is remaining.

7. In Exodus 3, Moses is summoned to the mountain by God. God tells Moses to remove his sandals because he is standing on holy ground. Moses is so overwhelmed, overjoyed and afraid at what this means, to be in the presence of God Almighty, that he covers his face because he is afraid to look at God.

8. Job 42:2 "I know that you can do all things, and that no purpose of yours can be thwarted." Job says this to God.

9. history.house.gov/Exhibitions-and-Publications/WIC/Historical-Essays/No-Lady/Womens-Rights (accessed February 3, 2017)

10. doloreshuerta.org/dolores-huerta (accessed March 3, 2017)

11. biography.com/people/constance-baker-motley-9416520 (accessed March 3, 2017)

12. beliefnet.com/inspiration/2010/01/inspiring-quotes-from-great-women-in-history.aspx?p=8 (accessed March 3, 2017)

# About the Author

Yvette R. Blair-Lavallais was seven-years-old, sitting in the pew at Lee Chapel AME Church in Dallas, when she sensed that God was calling her to preach. She asked her parents if she could be baptized because she wanted to follow the life of Christ that she heard and read about in Sunday School. Yvette has a passion for serving God's people and leading them from brokenness to wholeness. She enjoys teaching and preaching God's word and developing Bible study curriculum.

She is a licensed pastor and elder in the United Methodist Church and most recently served as the Associate Pastor of Congregational Care at First United Methodist Church in Lewisville, and was the first African American clergy in that church's 130-year history. Additionally, she has served as the Associate Pastor of Discipleship at the historic St. Luke "Community" United Methodist Church in Dallas, where she led the Women's Ministry, helped created and led the Isaiah 6:8 Young Adult Ministry, e2 Wednesday Night Worship (Elevate Your Worship Experience), and directed the Zan Wesley Holmes Servant Leadership Institute. She also served as an Associate Pastor at The Woods United Methodist Church in Grand Prairie.

A 2013 Magna Cum Laude graduate of Perkins School of Theology at SMU, Yvette earned a Master's of Theological Studies degree with a concentration in Church History. She was actively involved in campus community life and served as president of the student body, vice-president of the Black Seminarians Association and as editor-in-chief of the *Perkins Student Journal*. She and her husband launched and hosted "*Jumpstart Gospel Praise & Worship*," a weekly worship service for young adults at SMU.

Yvette is a native of Dallas and has more than 25 years of experience in media, corporate communications, public relations and non-profit, including receiving a congressional appointment to serve as the Public Relations Specialist at the Smithsonian Institution in Washington, DC. Before going into full-time ministry, Yvette served for three years as the Regional Vice President of Communications and Marketing for the South Central Affiliate of the American Heart Association, the first African American to hold that position.

Yvette also holds a BA in Journalism from the University of North Texas. She is the founder of "*From Brokenness to Wholeness*" Women's Conference, where women receive hope and healing through prayer, empowerment and transformative teaching. She is also the founder of *Her Sister's Situation*, a ministry for women who are dealing with an issue or combination of circumstances at any given time. By coming together and being a P.E.E.R. to one another, no sister has to suffer alone. This ministry was born out of her own experience of being a survivor of sexual harassment/assault.

Yvette is a 2017 fellow of Princeton Theological Seminary's Black Theology and Leadership Institute. She and her husband, the Rev. Carl Lavallais, live in Dallas.

Learn more about speaking engagements, Bible study curriculum and opportunities for Yvette to share at your church or event. Visit yvetteblair.com and follow her on Twitter @ damselfly_faith and on Instagram at preachergirl716.